RACE TO THE
RHINE

LIBERATING FRANCE & THE LOW COUNTRIES

RACE TO THE RHINE

LIBERATING FRANCE & THE LOW COUNTRIES

Leo Marriott & Simon Forty

Abbreviations & Glossary

2TAF 2nd Tactical Air Force
AA/AAA anti-aircraft (artillery)
AB airborne
Abt *Abteilung* (battalion-sized unit)
APC armored personnel carrier
ATk anti-tank
Bde brigade
Bty battery
CCA/B/R Combat Command A/B/Reserve
Cdo Commando
CG commanding general
CoS Chief of Staff
CWGC Commonwealth War Graves
   Committee
DLI Durham Light Infantry
DSC Distinguished Service Cross
DZ/LZ Drop zone/Landing zone
ECB engineer combat battalion
ETO European Theater of Operations
FA field artillery
FJR *Fallschirmjäger* = para
Flak *Flugzeugabwehrkanone* = AAA
G/PIR glider/parachute infantry regiment
GOC general officer commanding
IED improvised explosive device
KOSB King's Own Scottish Borderers
KwK *Kampfwagenkanone* = tank gun
LVT landing vehicle tracked
LST landing ship tank
Mecz mechanized
Mot motorized
MKB *Marine Küsten Batterie* = naval
   coast battery
OB West *Oberbefehlshaber West* =
   C-in-C West
PaK *Panzerabwehrkanone* = ATk gun
PIAT projectile infantry anti-tank
PLUTO pipeline under the ocean
PzGr *Panzergrenadier* = armored infantry
RAMC Royal Army Medical Corps
RASC Royal Army Service Corps
RTR Royal Tank Regiment
S-mine *Schuh-mine* = anti-personnel
   mine
SdKfz *Sonderkraftfahrzeug* = special
   purpose vehicle
SHAEF *Supreme Headquarters Allied
   Expeditionary Force*
sPzAbt *schwere Panzer-Abteilung* = heavy
   tank detachment
Stp *Stützpunkt* = strongpoint
StuG *Sturmgeschütz* = assault gun
TAC Tactical Air Command
TCC Transport Combat Command
USAAF US Army Air Force
VGR *Volksgrenadier* = late war German
   infantry unit
WN *Widerstandsnest* = pocket of
   resistance

Published in the United States of America and Great Britain in 2014 by
CASEMATE PUBLISHERS
908 Darby Road, Havertown, PA 19083
and
10 Hythe Bridge Street, Oxford, OX1 2EW

Copyright 2015 © Leo Marriott & Simon Forty

ISBN-13: 978-1-61200-294-1

Produced by Greene Media Ltd.,
34 Dean Street, Brighton BN1 3EG

Cataloging-in-publication data is available from the Library of Congress and the British Library.

10 9 8 7 6 5 4 3 2 1

Printed and bound in China

For a complete list of Casemate titles please contact:

CASEMATE PUBLISHERS (US)
Telephone (610) 853-9131, Fax (610) 853-9146, E-mail: casemate@casemate-publishing.com

CASEMATE PUBLISHERS (UK)
Telephone (01865) 241249, Fax (01865) 794449, E-mail: casemate-uk@casemate-publishing.co.uk

Page 1: *The Todt Battery on Cap Gris Nez symbolized the threat of the Atlantic Wall.*

Page 2–3: *Stützpunkt von Kleist, between Vlissingen and Koudekerke on Walcheren, was made up of four bunkers, two R611s (inner pair) and two R669s for 155mm guns.*

Below: *Battery Oldenburg near Calais. See page 52.*

CONTENTS

INTRODUCTION: BREAKOUT

Below: *The Germans had bottled up the Allies for some weeks after the landings, but at great cost. The buildup of men and materiel from across the Channel, the incessant air attacks, and continuous fighting played their part in reducing German reserves. When the Allied breakout came, the Germans could do little to contain the damage. Argentan, severely damaged by the fighting, was liberated on August 20 by US 80th Inf Div.*

Right and Below Right: *Fortunately Mont St. Michel survived the war unscathed and there are few discernable differences between these then and now photos.*

Above: *By Fall 1944 the Low Countries had endured four years of occupation by the Germans during which time they suffered from stringent rationing, forced movement of workers to Germany—some 375,000 Belgians served in labor programs within Germany during the war, on top of the 200,000 PoWs captured in 1940—and an army of occupation. Unsurprisingly, they welcomed the Allies as liberators and accepted the collateral damage.*

Below: *Operation Cobra in full swing. After the initial bombing, by July 28, the German defenses across the US front had largely collapsed, and the rush to the Seine was underway.*

At dawn on June 6, 1944, Allied naval forces began landing troops on the beaches of Normandy on the north-west coast of occupied France. Preceded by airborne assaults, over 150,000 men and their equipment supported by tanks and armored vehicles were ashore at the end of the day. Operation Overlord was an outstanding success, but it might have been a different story if German forces had been poised to counterattack the landings even before they were clear of the beaches—as Rommel had recommended—or if the divisions held in reserve had been committed immediately. As it was, after years of planning the Allies were ashore in northwest Europe in sufficient strength to hold and reinforce the beachhead over the next few weeks. "Overlord," of course, was not an end in itself but only the first step in a campaign intended to finish the war in Europe by defeating the German Army in the field and striking into the very heart of the Fatherland.

In the days and weeks after D-Day, the strategic emphasis was to maintain the flow of troops and supplies to build-up forces ashore at a greater rate than the Germans could bring in new divisions to counterattack. This was not achieved without difficulty as bad weather, which blew up on June 19 and lasted for several days, destroyed the US Mulberry harbor and severely damaged the British one at Arromanches. Nevertheless, by the end of June the British and Canadians had 11 divisions ashore and the Americans 15. Ranged against them were approximately 20 German divisions including no fewer than seven Panzer divisions opposing the British sector around Caen. It was around this city that some of the bitterest fighting of the Normandy campaign took place with heavy casualties on both sides. The British commander, General Bernard Montgomery, has come in for heavy criticism for an apparent failure to make headway. Much of this is due to the fact that Caen, one of the objectives of D-Day itself, was not captured until July 9, over a month later. By that date it had been reduced to an unrecognizable pile of rubble, mostly due to heavy attacks by RAF Bomber Command on June 6 and again, this time with 467 Lancasters and Halifaxes, on the night of July 7.

However, although the British and Canadian forces around Caen had not made any significant advances, they had exacted a heavy price on the German forces ranged against them. They had also held down units which could have been used elsewhere— this was particularly noticeable when

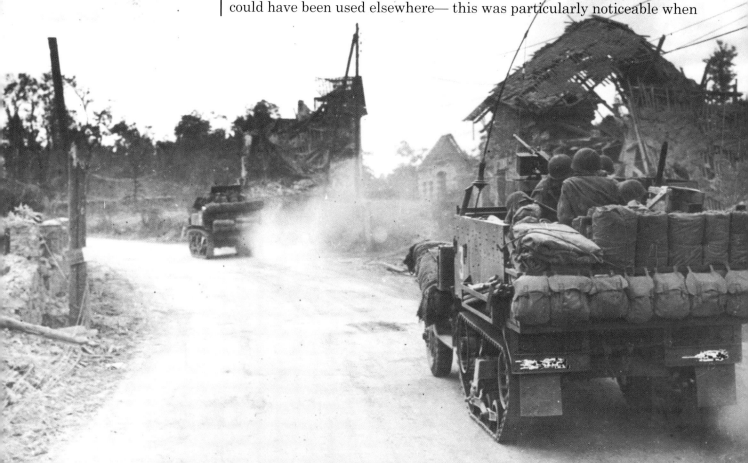

compared to the forces ranged against the American First Army under General Bradley on the right of the line, where by June 18 the US 9th Infantry Division had fought its way across the Cotentin peninsula thus isolating the German forces defending the approaches to Cherbourg which was captured on June 26. Subsequently, Bradley began a slow general advance to the south, hampered by stiff German resistance in the notorious Normandy bocage, a series of lanes and thick hedges which provided excellent concealment for defensive positions. By mid-July the US First Army had captured the town of St. Lô, an important point at a junction of several major roads.

In the meantime Montgomery had launched several major offensives which had met with only limited success but had pushed the British front forward by a few miles in each, gradually enveloping Caen. These included Operation Epsom which began west of Caen on June 26 but, opposed by six Panzer divisions, ground to a halt on July 1 having cost 6,000 casualties and numerous tanks. The Germans, however, had also suffered badly and a less cautious approach by the British commanders might have produced a more favorable outcome. Another, much larger, operation was

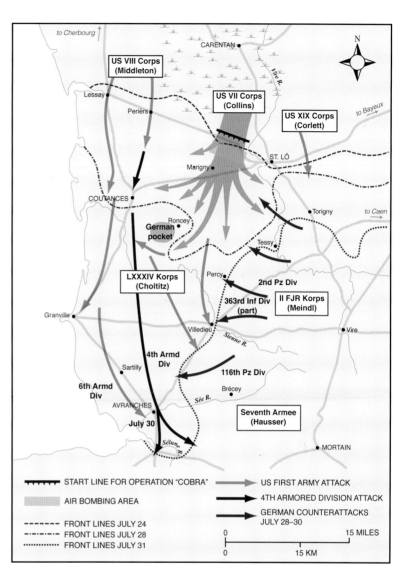

Above: *Operation Cobra and the German counterattack, Operation Lüttich (Liege).*

Operation Goodwood which was launched on July 18. From starting points to the east of Caen three armored divisions with over 800 tanks made a massed assault, supported by Canadian divisions moving through and to the west of the city. There were high hopes that this would prove to be the elusive breakthrough and to that end around 2,600 RAF and USAAF bombers went in ahead of the assault, carpet-bombing the German positions. However, the hoped for success was not achieved mainly due to traffic congestion caused by a poorly mapped (British) minefield and on the second day bad weather reduced available air support. This all gave the Germans time to regroup and literally hundreds of British tanks were picked off by the deadly 88mm anti-tank guns. By the time the offensive halted on July 20, British and Canadian casualties amounted to over 5,500. It was small consolation that Caen had finally been taken and the front line pushed forward a few miles.

Operation Cobra

In the meantime the US First Army was preparing for what would eventually become the major breakthrough of the Normandy campaign, Operation Cobra, which was launched on July 25. Its ultimate objective was the town of Avranches on the west coast at the base of the Cotentin peninsula. If a breakthrough could be made here, US forces could spread out to the west towards Brittany and Brest, and more importantly, swing east to cut behind the German forces ranged against the Allied line from Caen, through Caumont to St. Lô. Initial progress was slow but on August 1 the US Third Army was activated under the command of General

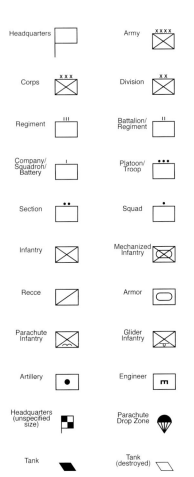

Headquarters		Army	
Corps		Division	
Regiment		Battalion/ Regiment	
Company/ Squadron/ Battery		Platoon/ Troop	
Section		Squad	
Infantry		Mechanized Infantry	
Recce		Armor	
Parachute Infantry		Glider Infantry	
Artillery		Engineer	
Headquarters (unspecified size)		Parachute Drop Zone	
Tank		Tank (destroyed)	

Opposite, Above: *War artist Harrison Standley's view of the wreckage in the Falaise Pocket, France, 1944. Standley documented US First Army's war, first in Ireland and England before going to France and then subsequently on to the Rhine.*

Opposite, Below: *Refugees are a terrible and inevitable part of war, often getting caught up in the action as they search for somewhere safe away from the fighting.*

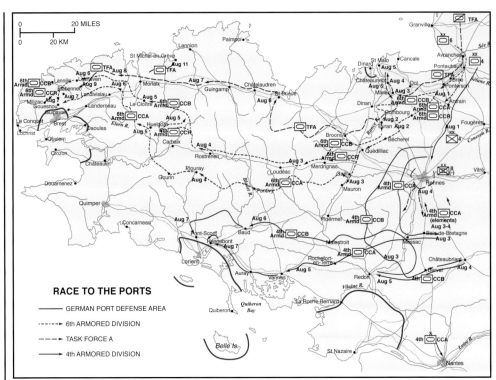

RACE TO THE PORTS

——— GERMAN PORT DEFENSE AREA

········ 6th ARMORED DIVISION

– – – TASK FORCE A

——— 4th ARMORED DIVISION

George Patton who had arrived in France on July 6 with his staff. Together with the already established First Army this now formed the US 12th Army Group under Bradley, with General Hodges taking over the First Army. Although at this stage Montgomery retained nominal command of all Allied land operations, the establishment of a US Army Group alongside his own 21st Army Group put the Americans on an equal footing and as the year went on the numbers of US divisions would outstrip the number of British and Canadian units in the north-west Europe campaign.

The vital breakthrough at Avranches was finally achieved on July 31 by the US 4th Armored Division, which became part of Patton's Third Army. It was planned that Patton would then swing westward into Brittany with the object of securing ports at Brest, Lorient, and St. Nazaire. However, Patton recognized that this was a waste of resources and after some delay he was permitted to swing his forces round to the east, leaving only VIII Corps to continue into Brittany. Already the enterprising 4th Armored had reached Rennes and it was becoming obvious there was little to prevent a general advance from there direct to Paris.

As American troops approached Avranches, Montgomery launched a new operation: "Bluecoat" directed towards the town of Vire close to boundary with the US First Army. Preceded by a heavy bombing attack the results were again mixed and the British VIII Corps was subsequently diverted eastward so that it was US forces which eventually captured Vire on August 6, while the British XXX Corps captured the important Mont Pincon on the same day. All this action served to tie down German forces which could otherwise have opposed the widening American breakout to the west.

On Hitler's direct orders, Generalfeldmarschall Günther von Kluge managed to muster four Panzer and two infantry divisions, together with supporting elements, with which to mount a counterattack. This was launched on the night of August 6, a westward thrust towards Avranches centered around the town of Mortain. If successful this would have split the US forces and re-established the German front line to the coast. Despite the fact that Ultra decodes provided some warning of the attack, the German panzers achieved some initial successes and made progress towards Avranches.

Initially fog and mist delayed the application of Allied air power but from around 11:00 Ninth Air Force P-47 Thunderbolts and RAF Typhoons

began to batter the German columns and stopped the
momentum of the advance. In particular the rocket-
armed Typhoons claimed to have destroyed dozens of
tanks, although post-battle investigations reduced the
confirmed total substantially. Nevertheless the aerial
onslaught effectively halted the German advance and
gave Bradley time to strengthen the American positions
and begin to launch his own counterattacks.
Although fighting continued for several days,
by August 13 the surviving German forces
withdrew having lost over 150 tanks

The Falaise Pocket

Even as the Germans were counterattacking at Mortain, Patton
was leading his Third Army in a
headlong rush to the east, passing
well south of Mortain. He had entered
Le Mans on August 8 having met
little opposition along the way. On
that day Montgomery launched the
Canadian Army southward from
Caen towards Falaise (Operation
Totalize)—although again a
cautious approach together
with a spirited counter-
attack meant that little
progress was made. To
the south Patton was
ordered to divert his XV
Corps which included the
Free French 2eme Division
Blindée (armored division)
northward toward Argentan,
about 15 miles south of Falaise,
which was reached on 13th. By

The pressure exerted on the German forces following the invasion came to a peak between August 12 and 21, 1944, in the aftermath of the abortive Operation Lüttich, the German counterattack at Mortain. Encircled by the Allies, the remnants of German Seventh Armee and Fifth Panzerarmee fought desperately to escape eastwards. Postwar historians have argued that the encirclement was poorly prosecuted, but the German losses were huge: some 10,000–15,000 killed and 40,000–50,000 taken prisoner. The equipment losses were also devastating: some 500 tanks and assault guns were lost in the pocket and much of what escaped did not cross the Seine. In full retreat, it would be logistics and resupply that hindered the Allies most as they chased the German forces through France. Eisenhower said,

"The battlefield at Falaise was unquestionably one of the greatest 'killing fields' of any of the war areas. Forty-eight hours after the closing of the gap I was conducted through it on foot, to encounter scenes that could be described only by Dante. It was literally possible to walk for hundreds of yards at a time, stepping on nothing but dead and decaying flesh."

Opposite, Below Right: *The Falaise Pocket.*

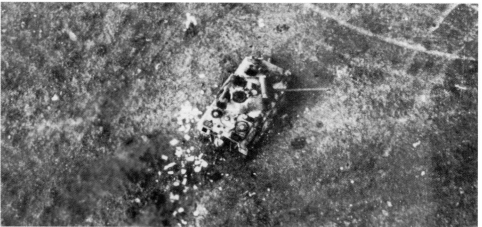

this time the German forces from the abortive Mortain offensive were retreating eastward and heading towards Falaise. Patton was eager to advance beyond Argentan but was ordered to halt as Falaise lay in the British sector of operations. Following the failure of "Totalize," another operation by the Canadian troops code-named "Tractable" began on August 13. Progress was slow against stubborn resistance and the difficulties in crossing the River Laizon but finally reached Falaise on the 16th.

By this time the German Seventh Armee and elements of the Fifth Panzerrmee to the west of the Falaise gap were being pressed from the north by the British Second Army and from south by US First Army. On the 19th elements of US Third Army now pressing northward met up with the Polish 1st Armored Division advancing southward ahead of the Canadian First Army. For the next couple of days the Allied strength was not enough to prevent scattered elements of shattered German units escaping through to the east, assisted by a counterattack by II Panzer Korps. Finally the gap was sealed on August 21 and with the trapped German units reeling under continuous and sustained air attack they quickly surrendered. For the Allies it was a substantial victory. The German Seventh Army had been destroyed and of the 80,000 troops caught in the encirclement some 10,000 were killed, and approximately 50,000 taken prisoner, the remainder managing to escape before the Allies could effectively seal the gap between Falaise and Argentan. In addition around 500 armored vehicles had been lost as well as thousands of B vehicles. Conditions inside the pocket were horrendous, the area littered with burnt out or abandoned vehicles and thousands of dead and dying strewn all over the area.

There has been much discussion about why some 20,000 Germans had managed to escape. The blame for this—as

Above Left: *The Polish 10th Cavalry Brigade, part of Polish 1st Armd Div in Canadian II Corps— seen deployed in open country south of Caen—was organized in France, many of its personnel being veterans of the 10th Mot Cav Bde who escaped the fall of Poland. It first saw combat on August 8 in the second phase of Operation Totalize, and was a part of the force that had the vital task of closing the Falaise Pocket.*

Above: *Polish Shermans wait to enter action on August 8. The attack, the first to use significant amounts of mechanized infantry, started well taking the Verrières Ridge but slowed down after a German counterattack by the 12th SS-Pz Div.*

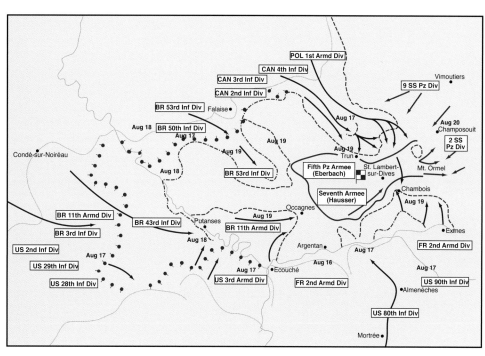

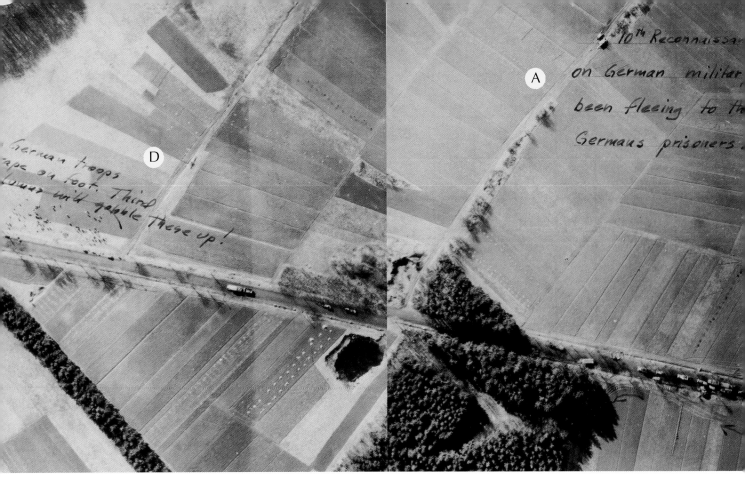

The text on the photo strip reads (handwritten):

A "...10th Reconnaissan... on German militar... been fleeing to th... Germans prisoners."

D "German troops ...ape on foot. Third ...mus will gobble these up!"

Air support comes in many guises, from artillery liaison and spotting, reconnaissance, medium and heavy bombing, and close support as exemplified here. Throughout the campaign in NW Europe, if the weather was good, Allied aircraft were on call and the Germans learnt to fear them—particularly the "Jabos." Here, the results of a fighter-bomber attack. The text on this recon photo strip reads:

A *10th Recon Gp photo strip of aftermath of XIXth TAC fighter-bomber attack on German military transport column in the vicinity of Limburg (M2398) which had been fleeing from the NE. Third Army troops later over-ran this area and took remaining Germans prisoner.*

B *These vehicles were all knocked out by strafing P-47s. Tanks or bulldozers must clear road before our mechanized columns can pass!*

C *Some vehicles were not destroyed and escaped after the attack by leaving the road.*

D *German troops escape on foot. Third Army columns will gobble them up.*

with much that is perceived to have gone wrong with the D-Day campaign—is usually laid at Montgomery's door, particularly by populist American authors. As is usually the case with these commentators, criticism tends to fall within national lines and it's instructive to remember that Bradley—who was there and dealing with the events—said, "George [Patton] was already blocking three principal escape routes through Alencon, Sees and Argentan. Had he stretched that line to include Falaise, he would have extended his roadblock a distance of 40 miles (64 km). The enemy could not only have broken through, but he might have trampled Patton's position in the onrush. I much preferred a solid shoulder at Argentan to the possibility of a broken neck at Falaise."

The victory of the Falaise Pocket represented the culmination of the Normandy battles in which the Germans lost over 450,000 men, over half killed or wounded, while the Allied ground forces suffered almost 210,000 casualties of which around 56,000 were killed or missing. In addition over 16,000 airmen lost their lives in operations connected with Operation Overlord and the Normandy battles.

Even while the Falaise battle raged, elements of Third Army pushed eastward to Paris. Lead elements of Gen. Philippe Leclerc's 2nd Armored Division entered on the evening of August 24. The German commander, General von Choltitz, formally surrende red the city the next day. Further north the Canadian First Army and British Second Army had also reached the River Seine at several points while the US V Corps had established a bridgehead across the river north of Paris. With German forces now falling back at all points of the front, the complete collapse of German strength seemed to have taken place and the Allies raced for the Rhine.

Air Support

A significant factor in the success of D-Day and the subsequent campaign in north-west Europe was the overwhelming air superiority which the Allies had gained by mid-1944. This in turn allowed tactical air forces to be deployed whose function was the close support of army operations on the ground with whom they worked in close co-ordination and co-operation.

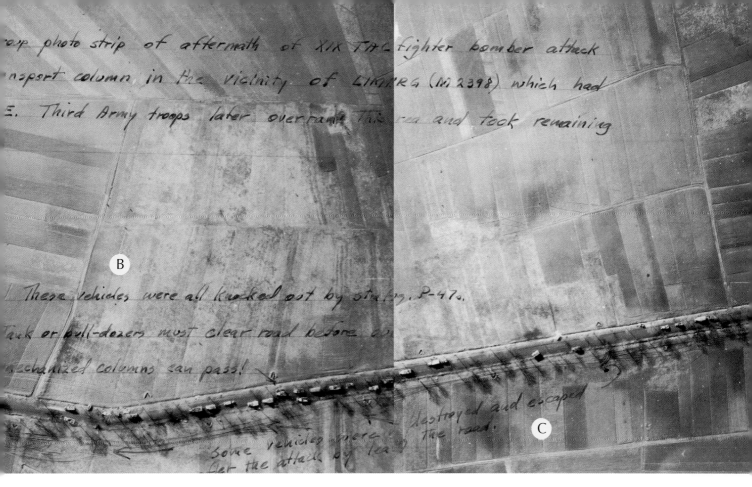

Historically, this had not always been the case and in the interwar years the RAF placed a low priority on what was termed "army co-operation" and failed to develop suitable aircraft and tactics tailor-made for the new era of Blitzkrieg warfare. The Luftwaffe honed its skills in the Spanish Civil War using dive bombers and fighters in direct support of ground troops in action and went on to utilize its hard-earned expertise in Poland, the Netherlands, France, Belgium, Greece, and finally Russia in a series of brilliantly conceived lightning campaigns.

It was in the fluid campaigns of the Western Desert in North Africa that the RAF began to evolve a method of working closely in support of the army. Army and air force commanders worked together at the highest levels, while on the ground RAF forward air controllers were integrated into mobile army units ready to call in air support whenever it was needed. It was found the fighters such as the Spitfire, Hurricane, and Curtiss Kittyhawk could be adapted to carry bombs, doing away with the need to develop specialist ground-attack aircraft. The "Cab Rank" system was introduced whereby squadrons and sections of fighter bombers would patrol over the battlefield ready to be called down to attack specific targets, often only yards away from their own forces. In addition the squadrons learned to become self-contained and completely mobile, moving from one airstrip to another at short notice as the front line ebbed and flowed. By 1943 when the North African campaign was concluded the system had been redefined and regularized and the ideas and tactics passed on to the nascent US Ninth Air Force which had cut its teeth in the North African desert alongside the RAF.

The conclusion of the North African campaign, followed by the invasion of Sicily and landings on the Italian mainland, freed up experienced units which relocated to the United Kingdom as part of the preparation for Operation Overlord. Already on June 1, 1943, the RAF had created the command structure for the 2nd Tactical Air Force (2TAF) which was intended to support the invasion and subsequent advance through north-west Europe. Subsequently, it became part of the Allied Expeditionary Air Force in the following November and comprised No. 2 Group (12 squadrons) equipped with medium bombers (Mosquito, Boston, Mitchell)

Above: *Typhoon of No. 440 Sqn, RCAF. Operational from March 30, 1944, the squadron supported ground units in the drive across Europe, carrying 500lb or 1,000lb bombs under each wing.*

Opposite, Top: *RAF Bomber Command and the USAAF provided significant bombing support during the Normandy campaign. However, large scale bombing was a double-edged sword—for both the civilians whose homes and livelihoods were destroyed and the soldiers underneath. Bombs are indiscriminate and there were many instances of what we would now call "blue on blue" events where Allied bombers bombed Allied positions. Heavy bombing also, in some cases, favored a well-entrenched defender because it made mobility of armor more difficult, However, there's no denying that the effect of bombardment by air and artillery did much to sap the morale of the defenders.*

and Nos. 83 and 84 Groups (each with 30 fighter-bomber squadrons as well as army co-operation squadrons flying Auster light aircraft). Aircraft flown by the fighter-bomber squadrons included Spitfires and Mustangs but the most significant type was the Typhoon. Carrying eight rocket projectiles each with a 60lb warhead these aircraft were highly effective against armored vehicles and tanks as well as soft-skinned targets such as trucks and railroad locomotives.

In October 1943 2TAF was joined by the US Ninth Air Force which had relocated from the Mediterranean Theater and by D-Day its order of battle included five fighter wings (P-51 Mustangs and P-47 Thunderbolts) and three bomber wings (A-20 Havocs and B-26 Marauders). Importantly it also had three troop carrier wings flying the ubiquitous C-47 Skytrain which, when not involved in airborne assault operations, flew continuous and vital supply missions. Confusingly, a USAAF Wing was approximately equivalent to an RAF Group while USAAF Groups were more akin to the British Wings, each consisting of three or four squadrons. The majority of the fighter units were equipped with the large and rugged P-47 Thunderbolt, affectionately referred to as the "Jug." Its air-cooled radial engine was less susceptible to damage from ground fire than the liquid-cooled Merlin which powered the P-51 Mustang, while the latter had a much longer range and better performance at altitude. Consequently, the Thunderbolt tended to be allocated to the ground-support missions while the Mustangs, while also used in that role, tended to be allocated escort missions with the bombers.

In the advance through north-west Europe these Allied tactical air forces provided the cover which enabled Allied ground forces to move almost at will, whereas the German Wehrmacht risked annihilation from the air if it tried large-scale movements by day. Consequently the Germans were restricted to movements at night or in periods of bad weather when Allied aircraft were grounded or unable to operate. No more clearly was this illustrated than in the Battle of the Bulge in mid-December 1944. Under cover of bad weather the Germans broke through the American lines, isolating the garrison at Bastogne, and pushing a salient deep into Allied territory. Despite heroic resistance on the ground and some determined counterattacks, the balance only finally swung back to the Allies when the weather cleared up after a few days and allowed the Allied air forces to range unopposed over the battlefield.

Although direct support of ground operations by 2TAF and the Ninth Air Force produced immediate and obvious results, the role of the strategic bomber forces (RAF Bomber Command and US Eighth Air Force) cannot be ignored. From May until the end of September 1944 these forces came under the direct command of Eisenhower as Supreme Allied Commander Europe and in the lead up to D-Day were heavily involved in the destruction of road and rail systems to isolate the invasion area. On D-Day itself and several subsequent occasions they were called in to provide direct support to battlefield operations, although the results were not always helpful. However, even after September when Air Marshal Harris and General Spaatz were able to resume their strategic bombing campaign, this still provided significant, if indirect, support to ground operations. The German transport network was constantly hammered so that troop movements were obstructed, and armament factories were targeted, although in fact German production output managed its peak in late 1944. However the most important bombing campaign was again German oil production (refineries, oilfields, synthetic oil plants) and the results of this were felt at all levels. German attacks were frequently halted or not even mounted due to lack of fuel and Luftwaffe operations were increasingly restricted for the same reason.

Naval Support

The naval element of Overlord, code-named Operation Neptune, was the largest operation of its type ever undertaken and involved 1,213 warships quite apart from the several thousand assault vessels ranging from tank landing ships right down to small landing craft and barges. Without the meticulously planned naval operation the landings could not have taken place. Once the troops were ashore the emphasis moved to protecting the beach-head and swarms of vessels offshore from air, surface, or submarine attack. In addition, well after D-Day the bombarding cruisers and battleships supported many inland operations with accurately targeted naval gunfire. A notable example of this was the capture of Cherbourg

Below: *P-47 Thunderbolt of 354th Fighter Gp, Ninth Air Force taxying at Rosieres en Haye in February 1945. This unit operated in support of US ground forces during the Battle of the Bulge. The P-47 was piloted by Maj. Glenn Eagleston, Ninth Air Force's highest scoring ace. The airfield, Advanced Landing Ground A-98, became a Ninth Air Force operational strip on November 21, 1944.*

where an American-led task force consisting of three battleships and four cruisers (including two British) mounted an effective bombardment of gun batteries and fortified positions which greatly aided the capture of the port by the US First Army. As the battle front moved away from the Normandy beach-head there was less call for bombarding ships, although some continued to support the advance up the Channel coast. Past Dunkerque and along the Belgian coast the offshore waters were very shallow and littered with treacherous sandbanks, consequently large ships could not operate close inshore and heavy fire support, where required, was provided by shallow draft monitors, many dating from World War I and typically mounting two 15in guns in a single turret.

As the various Channel ports were captured they were not of immediate use as the Germans had usually destroyed all the facilities and often sabotaged the harbor and its approaches with sunken blockships. It fell to naval salvage teams to sort out the mess and make the ports usable again, a job made infinitely more dangerous by numerous and ingenious booby traps left by the Germans. At Cherbourg, for example, it was three weeks after its capture before the outer harbor could be used and cargoes had to be taken ashore in DUKWs and small landing craft; and it was not until September that the inner port and its jetties were available.

Due to the speed of the British and Canadian advance after the breakout from Normandy, the valuable port of Antwerp was captured on September 6, totally surprising the German garrison forces who had no time to set about the destruction of the port which was taken virtually undamaged. However it was of no practical use until the German forces on either side of the approaches through the Scheldt estuary could be dislodged. The south bank was in Allied hands by October 24 but in order to clear the northern shore at Walcheren, a major naval operation had to mounted. Carried out in bad weather and commencing on November 1, it was supported by gunfire from the battleship HMS *Warspite* and the monitors HMS *Erebus* and *Roberts*. The amphibious force comprised no fewer than 181 landing craft and motor launches, many of which were sunk or seriously damaged in the operation which was eventually successfully completed a few days later.

In the meantime the immense task of clearing the estuary of mines —Operation Calendar—began on November 4 and the first supply ships were able to enter Antwerp on November 26. In three weeks of arduous

Below and Opposite: *Designed in the 1930s to be used in the Everglades and taken up by the USMC to be used in amphibious landings, the Landing Vehicle Tracked (LVT) came in various forms, including armored versions with turrets which were virtually amphibious tanks. They first saw action in the assault on Tarawa in late 1943, and by the end of the war had become an important part of the sophisticated armory used by US forces in the Pacific. LVTs found their way into the ETO in time to take part in the Battle of the Scheldt (as illustrated here), and in many river crossing operations. They were also extremely useful in the Low Countries after the dikes and dams had been breached and large areas of the countryside flooded.*

operations and hampered by bad weather, the minesweepers had swept or cleared no fewer than 267 mines to provide a safe approach channel.

Walcheren was the last major naval operation in support of the armies ashore, but early in 1945 a naval force consisting of 36 LCMs and 36 LCV(P)s was carried overland from Antwerp to Nijmegen where they were launched onto the Rhine. Originally they had been intended to assist in river crossing assaults but by the time they arrived in late March the 21st Army Group had already secured bridgeheads on the east bank. However they subsequently provided a valuable service, patrolling the river, assisting with the carriage of materials for bridge building and the LCMs actually took part in the successful assault on Arnhem on April 13.

Logistics

An essential element of the planning for Overlord was the buildup of troops, equipment, and supplies in the bridgehead following the initial landings. In reality this meant that by July 1 no fewer than a million men had been landed. They had to be fed and supplied, and the thousands of vehicles and aircraft required a continual flow of POL supplies. In the absence of an available port, the Allies brought their own in the shape of two prefabricated Mulberry harbors. These were up and running within a few days and by June 16, 1,500 tons a day was passing through each of them. Unfortunately, a gale blew up on June 19, which lasted for four days, effectively destroying the American Mulberry off Omaha and damaging the British one at Arromanches, although the latter was quickly repaired.

As the Allied buildup continued, the capture of established ports was a vital objective. Cherbourg was captured on June 28 but it was some time before it was brought into full-scale use. After the decision to move Third Army's thrust eastward instead of concentrating on capturing the Brittany ports of Brest, Lorient, and St. Nazaire—although the distances from Brittany to the Low Countries would have made resupply routes difficult—the capture of the Channel coast ports such as Le Havre, Boulogne, Calais, and Dunkerque became vitally important. This task was allocated to the Canadian First Army on the left flank of the Allied front, and after heavy fighting they were mostly available for use from the end of September—but their capacity was limited. A typical army division and its supporting elements required in total around 700 tons of supplies (including fuel)

Below: *A US convoy passes through the streets of Cherbourg after liberation. The Germans surrendered Cherbourg on June 26, and immediately 1056th Engineer Group, began reconstruction. By November 1, the port could unload 25,000 tons a day. Engineer Lt-Gen Emerson Itschner, who was a colonel in 1944 recemembered:*
"The Germans were kind enough to leave us a lot of very heavy steel beams, one meter in depth and up to 75 feet long. We had enough of these to bridge from the piles that we drove back to the seawall."
The beams came from Hadir in Differdange, Luxembourg. Itschner went to Differdange as soon as the town fell and soon after the factory was producing these meter beams which were put to many important uses, including building the railroad bridges across the Rhine.

every day. Until the opening of Antwerp on November 26, these supplies had to be brought by road or rail from the relatively small Channel ports. Most of these could only handle 5,000–10,000 tons per day, as against over 80,000 tons which Antwerp eventually was able to handle by December.

As the Allies advanced further into Europe and until Antwerp was available, the supply lines from bases and depots—still mainly in the Normandy area—were stretched further and further. Priority road supply routes were set up with convoys of lorries operating on a 24-hour schedule, the US route being well known as the Red Ball Express while the British equivalent was the Red Lion route. An important element in the supply network was the activities of the IXth Troop Carrier Command and No. 46 Group, RAF For example in a four-week period from late August to mid-September (when the aircraft were required for Operation Market Garden) over 23,000 tons was flown in of which 2,600 tons went to assist the civilian population in Paris.

Apart from food, ammunition and general supplies, the overwhelming need was for fuel oil. As part of the follow up to D-Day flexible oil pipes were laid across the English Channel, initially to Cherbourg but later to other points along the Channel coast as the allies advanced. Code-named PLUTO, the system encompassed over a thousand miles of pipe with associated pumping stations in England to bring oil from ports such as Liverpool and Bristol to the Isle of Wight and Dungeness from where it was pumped across the Channel. On the European mainland the vital oil pipes followed the Allied advance, eventually reaching through Belgium and Holland into Germany. By the start of 1945 some 300 tons per day was being pumped across and this rose dramatically to almost 40,000 tons per day by the end of the war. This was staggering achievement and one without which the Allied advance would have ground to a halt long before reaching the Rhine.

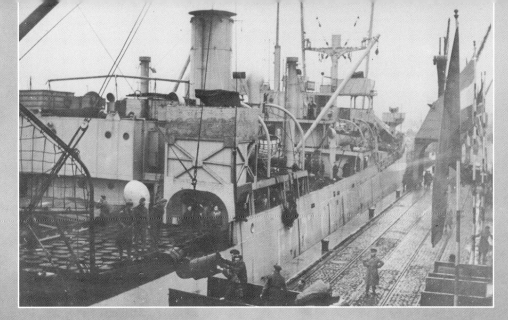

Main photo: *Minesweepers at rest after sweeping the Scheldt channel. Between November 3 and 25 Operation Calendar saw British minesweepers clear over 250 mines from the western Scheldt, clearing the approaches to Antwerp for safe use.*

Inset, Above: *On November 28, 1944, the Scheldt was opened for shipping and the Canadian-built Fort Cataraqui had the honor of being the first ship to berth at the Belgian port. Clearing the coast—the southern Breskens pocket, Walcheren, and South Beveland held by the German Fifteenth Armee—took six weeks and heavy casualties: 12,873 men of First Canadian Army (703 officers and 12,170 ORs) killed, wounded, or lost in action presumed dead. This photo shows oil being unloaded from the Fort Cataraqui.*

Inset, Center: *Within two weeks of opening the Scheldt, 19,000 tons of supplies were being unloaded at Antwerp each day.*

Inset, Below: *Canadian mine-sweeper returning to Antwerp. The impressive building with the tower is the Pilotage Building.*

By November 1944, 210,209 African Americans were serving in Europe. 93,292 of them were in the Quartermaster Corps.

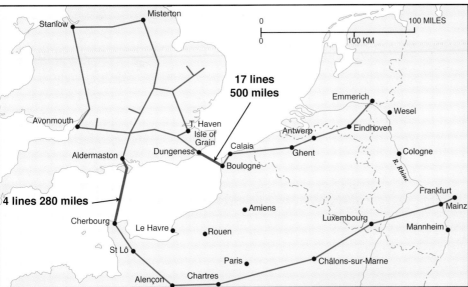

17 lines
500 miles

4 lines 280 miles

Supplying the Allied armies as they raced across France and northwest Europe was a major headache for the logistics staff. Tactical use of air drops (left, a container dropped in Oosterbeek during Market Garden)were certainly helpful to beleaguered troops in the field ... if they reached their intended recipients. The 426th Airborne QM Company provided five aerial resupply drops during Operation Market Garden, but of the supplies dropped, over 70 percent fell either into German hands or inaccessible terrain. However, in the critical days at Bastogne, improved pathfinder operations ensured a greater than 90 percent success rate. Airdropping was out of the question for larger units, and Eisenhower's broad-front approach meant that supplies had to reach four armies in the field. Until Antwerp was opened up most of what was needed had to be trucked from the Normandy beaches. The first PLUTO was laid on August 12, 1944, from the Isle of Wight to Cherbourg; later lines were laid from Dungeness to Ambleteuse in the Pas-de-Calais. These lines proved a major contribution to the Allies and by VE-Day over 172 million imperial gallons of gasoline had been pumped from Britain to France.

A huge trucking operation—the "Red Ball Express"—started rolling in August 1944 as the US Army Transportation Corps provided their troops with supplies, at its peak over 400 miles to the First Army and 350 to the Third. Most of those involved—as seen in the photos opposite of 4185th Quartermaster Service Coy in Liege, Belgium—were African Americans and they did a superb job. Nearly a thousand trucks— where possible observing a 60-yard interval and driving at 25mph—made a round trip that could last as long as 54 hours, no matter the weather or driving conditions, day and night (**Bottom Left**). The drivers also had to put up with enemy attack. The Red Ball Express truckers delivered 412,193 tons of gas, oil, lubricants, ammunition, food and other essentials.

Bridging

The Allied advance was constantly impeded by the complex network of waterways throughout northern France, Belgium, and the Netherlands. Apart from the major rivers—the Seine, Meuse (Maas), Waal, and Rhine—there was an extensive network of canals some of which were major waterways in their own right, the Prinz Albert Canal running eastward from Antwerp being a notable example. All of these formed natural defensive lines which had to be crossed and bridges became focal points in the campaign.

The Germans realized the importance of river crossings and almost every bridge, large or small, was fitted with demolition charges so that it could be destroyed. On top of this, of course, the Allies had destroyed many of the bridges before D-Day to interrupt German reinforcements and resupply. Consequently, it was rare to capture an intact bridge and so great reliance was placed on engineers in the Allied armies.

Where a bridge was totally destroyed, or even where none had existed previously, temporary bridges needed to be erected as quickly as possible. A variety of techniques were available. If the river was shallow, bulldozers were used to push stones into the river bed to create a temporary ford. Deep anti-tank ditches were another obstacle and these were filled with bundles of strong wood (fascines) which were carried and dropped by modified tanks. However, the best-known technique for crossing rivers was the construction of a Bailey bridge. Named after its inventor, a British civil servant, its great merit was that it was constructed of precision-engineered standard parts which could be transported and lifted into place without the need for heavy lifting equipment. Although a simple single-span bridge could be built to cross a narrow river or canal, wider waterways required the use of pontoons anchored in midstream to support a series of spans. First used it North Africa in 1942, the Bailey bridge system was licensed to American companies and was used extensively by the US Army in northwest Europe.

Opposite, Above: *Typical of the problems facing the Allies as they crossed Europe—here, the Wilhelmina Bridge over the Maas in Maastricht has been demolished by the retreating Germans when US 30th Inf Div reached the city.*

Opposite, Center and Below: *Single-span Bailey bridges in the Ardennes.*

Above Right: *Men of the Hampshire Regiment cross the Seine at Vernon on a hastily built bridge.*

Center Right and Right: *Anti-tank ditches that led to a number of portable bridging devices, such as the fascine, seen here carried by a Churchill AVRE.*

Opposite, Above: *The experimental Mine Exploder T1E3 was adopted as the M1 Roller by the US Army, although it was universally known as the "Aunt Jemima," after a well known pancake mix, because the five 8ft disks on the two forward units looked like stacks of pancakes. Heavy (the exploder unit weighed over 52,000lb itself) and awkward, it often had to be pushed by another tank. Around 200 were built.*

Opposite, Center: *The Sherman Crab used flails to clear mines rather than the "Aunt Jemima's pressure." A postwar US official report compared the various mine exploders and rated the Crab most effective. This one is seen after Arnhem was taken, April 14, 1945.*

Opposite, Below: *Typical German mines—the Schuh 42 anti-personnel mine and the doubling up of Teller mines.*

Right: *This GI is laying an M1A1 anti-tank mine.*

Below Right and Far Right: *Today we call them IEDs; during World War II they were a constant source of concern. The monthly US Army* Intelligence Bulletin, *designed to inform soldiers of such things included much on boobytraps and mines, often involving S-mines as illustrated. Two examples:*

"At times they laid S-mines by the hundreds in dry stream beds, and covered the prongs with small pebbles, so that it was impossible for us to know they were there, inasmuch as the whole area was a mass of pebbles. The Germans also prepared booby traps by interlacing the trip wires in the branches and suckers of blackberry bushes. The average soldier would not have suspected the presence of wires at all."
More harrowing:
"I lost my right hand by picking up a German 'egg' grenade that I saw lying on the ground, with its pin apparently in. Feeling confident that it was safe, I went right ahead and picked it up. It hadn't occurred to me that fine piano wire might lead from the other end of the grenade to a stake sunk into the ground directly underneath."

Mines and Boobytraps

Mines are primarily a defensive weapon, sown to protect positions, inconvenience and slow-up infantry and tanks, and channel enemy attacks into killing zones. Millions of them were used by every participant in the war. They were effective, too. The US Army identified that mines were responsible for 2.5% of fatalities in combat and for 20.7% of tank losses.

The advent of the mine detector helped balance things for a while—but it wasn't long before undetectable, non-metallic mines were produced. In one Lorraine minefield US soldiers found over 10,000 mines made out of plastic or wood—impossible to detect with metal detectors.

The Germans—on the defensive from 1943 onward—used mines and IEDs regularly. Allied infantrymen learnt not to pick up items of booty without great care: Lugers, machine-pistols, personal items were all fair game for the retreating soldier ... and better the recipient was injured rather than killed because it added to the logistical problems.

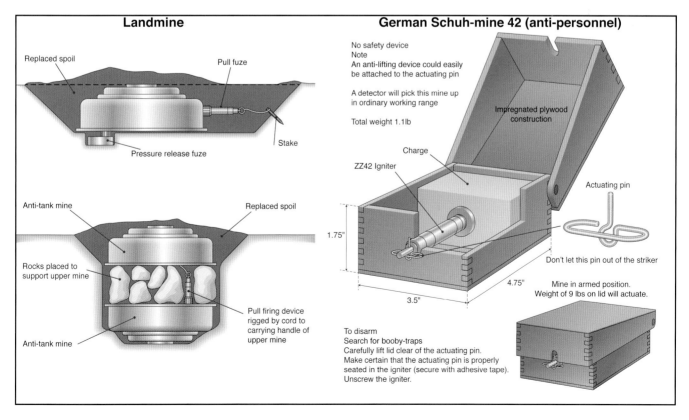

Landmine

Replaced spoil

Pull fuze

Pressure release fuze

Stake

Anti-tank mine

Replaced spoil

Rocks placed to support upper mine

Pull firing device rigged by cord to carrying handle of upper mine

Anti-tank mine

German Schuh-mine 42 (anti-personnel)

No safety device
Note
An anti-lifting device could easily be attached to the actuating pin

A detector will pick this mine up in ordinary working range

Total weight 1.1lb

Impregnated plywood construction

Charge

ZZ42 Igniter

Actuating pin

1.75"

Don't let this pin out of the striker

4.75"

Mine in armed position.
Weight of 9 lbs on lid will actuate.

3.5"

To disarm
Search for booby-traps
Carefully lift lid clear of the actuating pin.
Make certain that the actuating pin is properly seated in the igniter (secure with adhesive tape).
Unscrew the igniter.

1 THE ADVANCE ACROSS FRANCE

The great battle of Normandy had steamed like a pressure cooker for just over two months, but the pressure had been released and the German Army was blown away by the full power of the Allied buildup. Caught at Falaise, the remnants of the defenders of Normandy limped away from France most of their heavy weapons captured or destroyed. The *Rückmarsch* did not mean that they were incapable of putting up a fight, as the British who had to battle their way across the Seine at Vernon found out to their cost, but the speed and energy of the Allied advance gave the German forces little chance. It was during this time that the reliability and durability of the Allies' equipment showed its worth. Many commentators talk of the superiority of German equipment, particularly the Tiger tank: few Tigers could have advanced as far or as fast as the Allied M4s and Cromwells did in August and September 1944. In the north the Canadian First Army was tasked with clearing the Channel coast (see next chapter). The British Second and US First armies advanced over the Seine and into Belgium.

However, the grander stage was set for Patton who had been itching for a chance to bring mobile warfare to the ETO. Without a command after the slapping incident during the Sicily campaign, the most brilliant of the Allied generals had played little part in the grand alliance since then. Now was his chance ... and how he took it! After convincing his commander, Bradley, that Brittany was not the prize, his army moved into the exploitation phase after Operation Cobra had blasted a hole in the German lines. The Allied strategy, the lynchpin of which was the attrition of German panzer forces around Caen, had paid off and Georgie's boys were there to make sure that the Germans had no chance to regroup and set up a defensive line. After Falaise, Third Army pushed on toward the borders of Germany. Tight cooperation with the close air support group—XIX Tactical Air Command, commanded by Brig-Gen. Otto P. Weyland—and thrusting divisional commanders helped.

The tanks of Col. Bruce C. Clark's 4th Armored took Troyes at the gallop, then encircled Nancy allowing the city to be taken with little fighting, and then beat back a counterattack by the superior force of Fifth Panzerarmee at Arracourt. In 14 days of fighting 4th Armored's CCA had taken 1,884 PoWs, killed 589 of the enemy, destroyed 107 tanks, 30 SP guns, 32 guns, and 491 other vehicles.

At this untimely moment, the advance stopped: a shortage of fuel was the symptom, but the reason was that the Allies had outrun their logistic plan. They had moved more quickly than had been expected and there was no way to get fuel to the front. On September 25, Third Army ground to a halt. Then it started to rain: October and November were as wet as they could be.

On November 7 they got going again, but the Germans had used the breathing space to ensure Patton's next objective—Metz—would be no pushover. It would take Third Army a month and over 7,000 casualties to take the city whose circle of forts proved that even the most modern forms of warfare ended up in infantry slugging matches when confronted with such well-dug-in opponents. After Metz fell, Third Army continued into the Saar, advancing to the Westwall, which the army was about to attack when the Germans preempted this in the Ardennes.

WESTERN FRONT
September 1, 1944

Allied front line
Industrial areas
Main highways
Westwall
Trunk railroads

20 0 20 40 60
miles

N 13 | CALVADOS | N 13

CAEN

Crossing the Seine

After the breakout, the first major physical obstacle for the Allies was the Seine, a major waterway navigable by ocean-going vessels as far as Rouen. Slow-moving and wide in the west, in the east, against lighter opposition, Third Army took the river at a canter: 79th Inf Div found the Germans had abandoned Mantes-Gassicourt, northwest of Paris; 4th Armd Div crossed to the southwest at Troyes; 5th Inf Div crossed at Montereau; 7th Armd Div downstream from Melun— so, by August 25, Bradley's 12th Army Group had a number of bridgeheads over the Seine. Further west, where most of the German forces streaming back from Normandy were concentrated, the crossings were more keenly contested. At Vernon, the British 43rd Wessex Division had to cross 680ft of open water in an operation that author Ken Ford described as "lurching from crisis to crisis."

It was successful, however. At a cost of 560 casualties, BR XXX Corps had its bridgehead across the Seine. At Forêt de la Londe the Canadian 2nd Inf Div ran into the German 331st Inf Div and sustained nearly 600 casualties as the German rearguard fought valiantly to allow its troops to retreat across the Seine. Elsewhere, similar actions were taking place. At Criqueboeuf, the Algonquin Regt, part of the Canadian 4th Armd Div, crossed the Seine under fire from high ground (Hill 88) on the north bank. 3rd Div similarly seized a bridgehead at Elbeuf but not before large numbers of retreating Germans had crossed the Seine. While after the battle assessments suggested that the Germans had lost some 12,000 motor vehicles including 150 AFVs, Fifth Panzerarmee recorded 25,000 vehicles crossed the Seine between August 20 and 24, at night and under cover of bad weather. The Allies, the historians note, made one mistake: if Patton had exploited his Mantes-Gassicourt crossing by thrusting toward Rouen along the east bank instead of the west, fewer Germans would have escaped across the Seine. As it was he was ordered on the west, crossing the British Second Army front, and the moment passed.

A *Capt. Orville N. Fisher was a Canadian war artist, attached to the 3rd Inf Div, landing with them on the beach at Courseulles-sur-Mer. The only Allied war artist to land on D-Day, he made quick, on-the-spot sketches, later transferring to watercolors. This painting shows Sappers bridging the Seine at Elbeuf.*

B *A General Motors Staghound armored car of the XIIth Manitoba Dragoons crossing a Bailey bridge at Elbeuf, August 28. Soldiers are offloading railway ties to reinforce or smooth out the road surface.*

C *82nd ECB constructed this bridge over the Seine at Melun on August 30, supported by 17th Armd Engrs.*

D *The commander of the Canadian II Corps, Lt-Gen. Guy Simonds, watches Shermans of the Canadian Grenadier Guards (the 21st Canadian Armd Regt) cross the Seine at Elbeuf on August 28, from the vantage point of his staff car.*

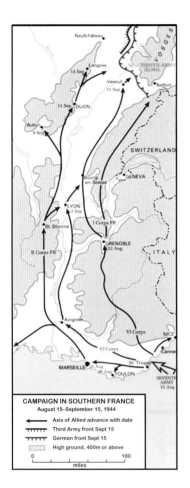

CAMPAIGN IN SOUTHERN FRANCE
August 15–September 15, 1944

⟵ Axis of Allied advance with date
Third Army front Sept 15
German front Sept 15
High ground, 400m or above

0 ————— 100
miles

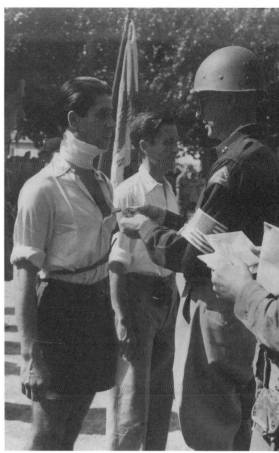

Operation Dragoon

On August 15 a second front was opened in France when the Allies assaulted the French Riviera by air and by sea. In a well-organized and efficient operation, US Seventh Army under Maj-Gen. Alexander Patch landed first followed by the French First Army. The subsequent march to the Vosges Mountains, the Germans fighting desperate rearguard actions all the way, saw the Seventh meet Patton's Third Army on September 10. The speed of the advance slowed as elsewhere— because of the problems of resupply, although when the port of Marseille came on stream it would supply over a third of Allied requirements in the last months of the war.

Above Left: *French Algerian troops rest alongside the road en route to the front.*

Above Right: *Maj-Gen Patch presents the Silver Star to Mr. Marc Rainaut leader of the FFI in Saint-Tropez, August 18.*

Right: *St. Maxime enjoys liberation.*

US Seventh Army fought its way through eastern France into Alsace-Lorraine, and on into Germany.

A Landing memorial at Pampelonne (Ramatuelle) near Saint-Tropez.

B The invasion fleet off Saint-Tropez.

C Seventh Army—in the form of French 2nd Armd Div—enter Strasbourg on November 23, 1944. The unit received a US Presidential Unit Citation for its work.

D Seventh Army arm patch.

E Seventh Army soldiers at the Westwall near Climbach, France, December 15. Halted while the Battle of the Bulge took place, Seventh Army extended westward as Third Army moved north and, subsequently, the two armies cleared the Saar-Palitinate triangle in spring 1945 (see pp150–151).

Liberating Paris

On June 14, 1940, German troops marched into Paris. On June 22 France surrendered and on June 25 Hitler toured the city with Albert Speer at his side. Just over four years later, on August 25, 1944, General der Infanterie Dietrich von Choltitz surrendered Paris and 17,000 men to French General Philippe Leclerc and the Resistance leader Henri Rol-Tanguy at the Gare Montparnasse. Choltitz had been in charge for less than a month and would claim to be the savior of Paris for refusing to follow Hitler's order to lay waste to the city. Charles de Gaulle (**B**), president of the Provisional Government of the French Republic, arrived shortly after and took over from the Vichy government which had been removed by the Germans and ended up in Sigmaringen in the Danube valley as an unlikely "government in exile." There was sniping, sporadic fighting in the city and an artillery bombardment in the following days, but the parade of US 28th Inf Div down the Champs Élysées (**A**) showed where the power lay. After the euphoria died down, Parisians began to come to terms with the realities of freedom.

Patton's Advance

A *Falaise falls to the Canadians on August 18.*

B and C *On September 13, less than a month after Operation Dragoon landed 9,000 airborne troops and 90,000 by sea, recon elements of 6th Armd from Patton's Third Army met French troops from Patch's Seventh in front of Autun's town hall (seen also today, **C**) suitably decorated with the Free French flag.*

E *Three of the big wheels: Patton, Bradley, and Montgomery. While historians may debate the details of the battles from their armchairs, the Allied commanders led the largest amphibious operation ever, destroyed the army in front of them, and reached the German border inside four months: a remarkable achievement.*

D *Gen. Philippe Leclerc (with mustache) lands in Normandy. His 2nd Armd Div played an important role in Patton's advance*

(Patton awarded Leclerc the Silver Star for a brilliant action against 112th Pz Bde) and as a figurehead for France. His men led the liberation of Paris and subsequently, as part of Seventh Army, Strasbourg—fulfilling an oath Leclerc and his men had made in the desert, the Oath of Kufra, in February 1941: "You shall not lay down arms, until the day when our colors, our beautiful colors, fly over Strasbourg Cathedral."

F *As it neared Lorraine, only fuel shortages seemed capable of stopping Third Army. At Verdun on August 31, a 400-mile advance from Normandy, XX Corps crossed the Meuse, but was already perilously close to running out of fuel. Further south, 4th Armored was ordered to advance until the tanks ran dry and then continue on foot. Third Army was spearheaded by XII and XX Corps, armored vehicles of the latter seen regrouping outside Chartres on August 17.*

G *By early September Third Army was at the Moselle. After stern fighting XII Corps had a bridgehead across the river. Here a jeep from CCB of 4th Armored passes a medical jeep of 35th Infantry.*

A and B *Third Army was spear-headed by XX and XII Corps.*

C *Maj-Gen. Manton S. Eddy, CG XI Corps, Lt-Gen. Patton, CG Third Army, and Maj-Gen. Walton H. Walker, CG XX Corps.*

D *Patton's end-of-war letter of commendation to Walton H. Walker for the fighting qualities of XX Corps, in particular the reduction of the Saar–Moselle triangle.*

E *This M4A1 (76mm) Sherman is a memorial to the fighting around Nancy, a ten-day battle which saw the city liberated and the Moselle and Meurthe river bridges secured.*

F *Metz memorial remembering liberation on November 22, 1944. "On this place general Walker, commander of the XX Corps of the Third Army of General Patton, transferred the city of Metz, which was liberated by his troops, to the French authorities."*

G *M4A4 commemorates the battle at Arracourt, where 4th Armored defeated a counter-attack by Fifth Panzerarmee.*

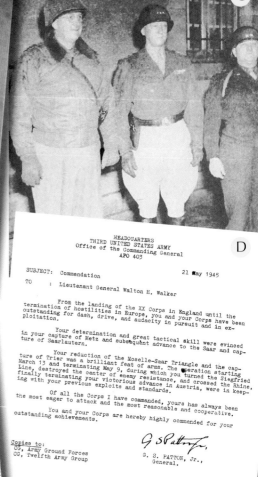

HEADQUARTERS
THIRD UNITED STATES ARMY
Office of the Commanding General
APO 403

SUBJECT: Commendation   21 May 1945

TO   : Lieutenant General Walton H. Walker

From the landing of the XX Corps in England until the termination of hostilities in Europe, you and your Corps have been outstanding for dash, drive, and audacity in pursuit and in exploitation.

Your determination and great tactical skill were evinced in your capture of Metz and subsequent advance to the Saar and capture of Saarlautern.

Your reduction of the Moselle-Saar Triangle and the capture of Trier was a brilliant feat of arms. The operation starting March 13 and terminating May 9, during which you turned the Siegfried Line, destroyed the center of enemy resistance, and crossed the Rhine, finally terminating your victorious advance in Austria, were in keeping with your previous exploits and standards.

Of all the Corps I have commanded, yours has always been the most eager to attack and the most reasonable and cooperative.

You and your Corps are hereby highly commended for your outstanding achievements.

Copies to:
CG, Army Ground Forces   G. S. PATTON, Jr.,
CG, Twelfth Army Group   General.

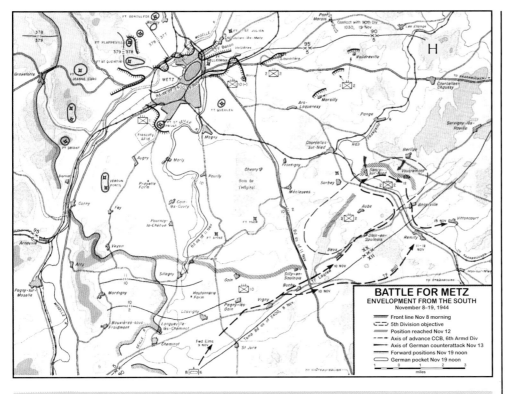

H *After the speedy progress across France, the battles first for Metz and then on to the German border saw Third Army involved in attritional warfare with heavy casualties on both sides. The attack on the well-defended city of Metz and its string of fortresses—the last of which held out until mid-December—typified the struggle. The city was taken eventually after attacks from the eastern side.*

BATTLE FOR METZ
ENVELOPMENT FROM THE SOUTH
November 8–19, 1944

Front line Nov 8 morning
5th Division objective
Position reached Nov 12
Axis of advance CCB, 6th Armd Div
Axis of German counterattack Nov 13
Forward positions Nov 19 noon
German pocket Nov 19 noon

1   0   1   2   3
miles

I *The battle of Metz started in late September but it was only on November 18 that US forces were able to enter the city. It capitulated on November 22, although the forts held out for longer.*

J *M10 tank destroyer in Metz.*

K *"Der Mann kann fallen, die Fahne nicht"*—men may fall, but the flag never! A Nazi slogan seen on a wall in Metz. The US Army Center of Military History's book on the Rhineland campaign by Ted Ballard noted:
"In incredibly harsh weather, over difficult terrain, and against a determined foe, Eisenhower's soldiers had triumphed ... In mid-December Eisenhower wrote to Ernie Pyle, the well-known war correspondent, that it was his foot soldiers who had demonstrated the 'real heroism—which is the uncomplaining acceptance of unendurable conditions.' At Aachen, at Metz, in the Huertgen Forest, in the Vosges Mountains, along the length of the Siegfried Line, and on to the Rhine River, the Allied infantryman had persevered and, through his determination, vanquished the Wehrmacht."

Right: *Between early September and mid-December the Allied armies advanced towards the Rhine, coming up against the great defensive structure of the Westwall. This had come under attack in Lorraine when the German offensive in the Ardennes started. Third Army stopped its own offensive and wheeled northward, relieving hard-pressed First Army positions in Belgium and Luxembourg.*

WESTERN FRONT
December 20, 1944

——— Allied front line 12:00 Dec, 20

▷ Axis of German counterattack

Westwall

– – – German front line Sept 5

20   0   20   40   60
miles

Above: *After Metz, the next stepping stones towards the Reich were the cities of the Saar—such as Saarlautern (now reverted to its original name Saarlouis) and Saarbrücken— whose defense was supported by the Westwall fortifications. This M10 tank destroyer was knocked out in the fighting at Saarlautern.*

Opposite, top left: *The Dillingen-Pachten Bridgehead was pushed across the Saar in early December and was the scene of vicious fighting around the bunkers and defenses of the Westwall. The Ardennes offensive halted the American push and the bridgehead was given up.*

Right: *The heights of Spicheren, southwest of Saarbrücken, did not fall until February 21, 1945, by which time it was part of Seventh Army's front. Men of US 70th Inf Div ("Trailblazers") took the village and in 1997 commemorated the event by placing an M24 Chaffee as a memorial.*

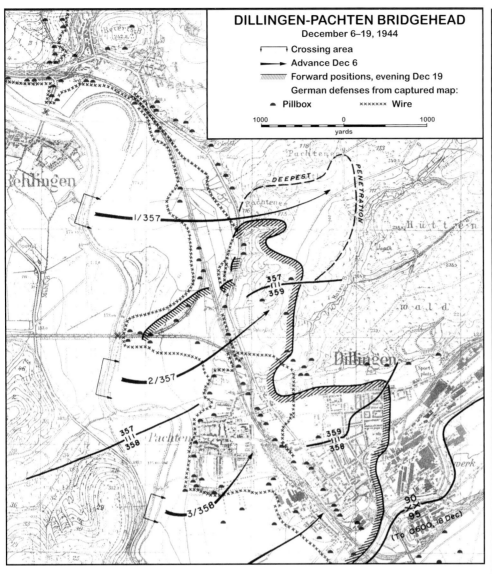

DILLINGEN-PACHTEN BRIDGEHEAD
December 6–19, 1944

⌐¬ Crossing area
➝ Advance Dec 6
▨ Forward positions, evening Dec 19
German defenses from captured map:
⏶ Pillbox   ×××××× Wire

1000   0   1000
yards

Rehlingen

DEEPEST PENETRATION

1/357

357
III
359

2/357

357
III
358

Dillingen

Pachten

3/358

359
III
358

90
××
95
(Tp 0600, 18 Dec)

MUNICIPAL SLAUGHTERHOUSE   PRIMS RIVER   TO SAARLAUTERN-RODEN

The Westwall surprised the Allies, who had not realized how complex it was, being built with interlocking bunkers and pillboxes, each with lines of fire that protected its neighbor. Additionally there were emplaced tank turrets, dragon's teeth anti-tank defenses, bunkers disguised as houses, and armored MG turrets. Dillingen and Pachten were particularly well defended as the photos on this page, taken in the area, show.

2 CLEARING THE FRENCH COAST

This view looks from close to the Belgian border toward Dunkerque along the famous beaches from which the British evacuated in 1940. (Ship remains can still be seen at low tide (**E**).) There are many Atlantic Wall sites along this stretch of coast, many of them superimposed on top of earlier French defenses. Visible here are MKB Malo Terminus (**A**), which was built on top of a French fort that has its origins in the 18th century. It and Fort des Dunes (**B**) were attacked and taken in June 1940. New bunkers and gun emplacements were built, four R671 casemates took first 9.4cm Vickers Armstrong guns which were replaced in June 1944 with 10.5cm guns. Fire control was provided by an M162a fire control post. Additionally there were various FlaK and other gun positions. Fort des Dunes became Funkmeßortungsstellung Dahlie. Just north of the battery is an R219 Doppelschartenstand (**C**), an anti-tank casemate with two firing positions. At (**D**) is the R636 command post for a coastal battery (8th Battery Artillery Regt 18) of four 15.5cm guns inland at Stp. Delphin.

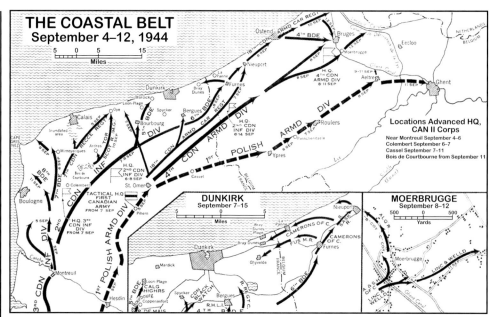

THE COASTAL BELT
September 4–12, 1944

Miles

Locations Advanced HQ,
CAN II Corps
Near Montreuil September 4–6
Colembert September 6–7
Cassel September 7–11
Bois de Courtbourne from September 11

DUNKIRK
September 7–15

Miles

MOERBRUGGE
September 8–12

Yards

Above: *Dieppe has a special place in the wartime memories of Canadians. It was here that 5,000 Canadians of the 2nd Inf Div, 1,000 British Commandos, and 50 US Rangers landed along with armored support in the form of The Calgary Regiment. The raid was a disaster: 3,367 Canadians were killed, wounded, or taken prisoner. The Commandos lost 247 men. The Royal Navy lost a destroyer, 33 landing craft, and 550 dead and wounded. The RAF lost 106 aircraft. The Germans had 591 casualties and lost 48 aircraft. After Dieppe fell to the Canadian 2nd Inf Div on September 1, there was much interest in the scene of the raid—here (Top) officers are seen examining destroyed German defenses above the narrow beach at Puits, that had been assaulted by the Royal Regiment of Canada. There was a memorial service in the nearby military cemetery to honor those who died in the raid. (Above) the Canadian Army Commander during the service.*

Montgomery's directive to Canadian First Army was to "operate northwards ... secure the port of Dieppe ... proceed quickly with the destruction of all enemy forces in the coastal belt up to Bruges ... One Corps will be turned westwards into the Havre peninsula, to destroy the enemy forces in that area and to secure the port..."

The Channel coast east from the mouth of the Somme was well defended—even more so than the stretch of Normandy the Allies attacked on June 6. The Germans had had four years to prepare for the attack, although the so-called Atlantic Wall was not started immediately. At first, from May 1940 to around October 1941, there were few fortifications, then British commandos raided the Lofoten Islands, sinking ships, destroying infrastructure, and taking captives.

The response was immediate: on October 4, 1941, Generalfeldmarschall Erwin von Witzleben, then Oberbefehlshaber West, issued orders to start building fortifications. Shortly after, Hitler issued an order for a significant construction program that would see a continuous line of defense from Norway to the Spanish border. Too much for the army engineers, the program was given to Organization Todt to accomplish. A further meeting in March 1942, led to von Rundstedt's August 25, 1942, directive for 15,000 bunkers from the Netherlands to Spain.

The sector from the Scheldt to the Somme estuary—the closest part of the coastline to Britain and a possible invasion—was defended by the Fifteenth Armee. This is where the main effort took place and building averaged a density of 11 bunkers per kilometer as compared to 4–8 elsewhere. After the breakout from the Normandy bridgehead, the Channel ports were of great importance to help supply the Allied armies in the field. In September Hitler declared the ports fortresses: the Canadians can attest to the strength of resistance encountered in many of these locations, although not in Dieppe, scene of the abortive raid in 1942, and Ostend.

Canadian First Army was a cosmopolitan affair made up of men from a number of nations, including British I Corps, 1st Polish Armored Division, 6th Airborne Division, 1st Belgian Infantry Brigade, and the Royal Netherlands Brigade (Prinses Irene)—although the Belgians moved to Second Army in September.

One by one the ports fell: Dieppe on September 1; Le Havre on September 12; Boulogne on September 22; Cap Gris Nez and Calais by September 30. Ostend was given up without a fight, but Dunkerque fought on and surrendered only on May 9, 1945, after having been contained for six months by the 1st Czechoslovak Armored Brigade.

Left: *The passage of time sees Hitler's Atlantic Wall falling into the sand. This one is south of Boulogne, part of Stp Obelisk. The two large bunkers are an R612 (**A**) Schartenstand für Land und Sturmgeschütze—a casemate housing a large weapon—and an R502 (**B**) Doppelgruppenunterstand— personnel bunker. To the left is a stand for a 5cm KwK (**C**).*

Below Left: *Le Havre was almost completely destroyed before the assault. 2,000 civilians died; 350 ships and 18 kilometres (11 mi) of docks, as well as 15,000 buildings were destroyed. Controversially, the request by German commander Col. E. Wildermuth that the French civilians should be evacuated from the city prior to the bombardment, was refused.*

Bottom: *Allied bombers visited Dieppe in April 1944: as with so many coastal towns, the RAF and USAAF battered docks and ports. Luckily for the inhabitants, the Germans left Dieppe without a fight, so the town did not receive the usual artillery bombardment.*

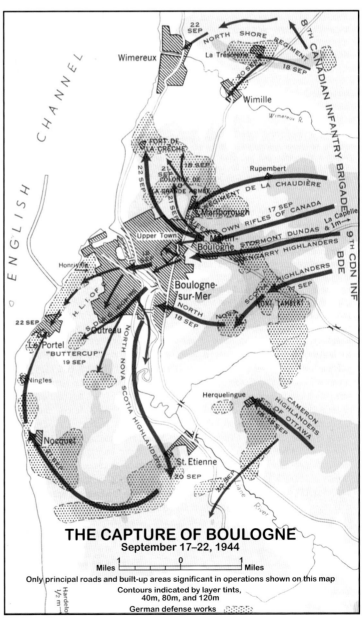

Boulogne

Hitler had declared Boulogne a fortess and it was defended by 10,000 men. Operation Wellhit saw Canadian 3rd Inf Div, supported by specialized armor from BR 79th Armd Div, take the city in a hard-fought action that lasted September 17–22. The harbor area had been destroyed on June 15, by an RAF raid that included Lancasters carrying "Tallboy" bombs, but this didn't stop a PLUTO oil pipeline being laid from Dungeness. This was operational from October 10.

Above: *An aerial view of a bombing run in progress on Mont Lambert, France. Capturing the village and its artillery positions was a key objective for Canadian forces and it was in their hands by nightfall of the first day of fighting.*

The Pas de Calais was as heavily defended a stretch of the Atlantic Wall as could be found, and the areas around Boulogne (this spread), Cap Gris Nez (see pp48–49), and Calais (see pp50–51) were studded with every type of emplacement possible. The three illustrated here show the variety: look at the brilliant http://www.atlantikwall.mynetcologne.de or http://www.bunkerpictures.nl for more information.

Above Right: Stp 265 Lungenkraut. Near the village of Equihen, south of Boulogne, are the remains of five unusual SK (Sonderkonstruktion = specially constructed) bunkers, part of Luftwaffe long-range navigation system FuG 121 Erika. There's another of these sites at Saint-Pierre-Eglise on the Cotentin peninsula. By listening to the transmissions from the two stations aircraft could work out their precise positions (to within 400m). There are a number of FlaK positions around the site.

Center Right: Between Equihen and Le Portel is Kriegsmarine Station Nessel. It has a V143 bunker which would have been equipped with a Mammut radar station. Mammut (Mammoth) was the world's first phased array early warning radar. Alongside the V143 are two R622 bunkers for the crew and, as shown here, six L401 bunkers that provided the Flak battery for the site (they could take 8.8cm or 10.5cm AA guns), with a command post in the middle.

Below: Stp 259 Pechnelke had four R671 emplacements, as well as a 9.4cm FlaK emplacement and a number of other personnel bunkers including a hospital bunker.

BATTERE TOU

Cap Gris Nez

You can't get much closer to England than Cap Gris Nez, and following the Fall of France in 1940, the Germans built a number of coastal gun batteries that could be used against shipping, to bombard Britain's south coast, and support the intended invasion. Between August 1940 and September 26, 1944—the day the final round was fired across the Channel—over a thousand shots rained down on Kent, killing more than 200 civilians and damaging over 10,000 properties. The capture of Calais and the batteries was accomplished in Operation Undergo by Canadian 3rd Inf Div between September 25–30. In spite of its "fortress" designation, Calais and the batteries did not fight to the last man and so Canadian casualties were lighter than anticipated.

Today, one of the four huge Battery Todt casemates, which housed 380mm guns, provides the setting for the Atlantic Wall Museum and—as can be seen in the photo below—outside the museum is a German Krupp K5 railway gun. The battery—originally named MKB (Marine Küsten Batterie) Siegfried—was completed in January 1942 by Organization Todt, the labor movement named for Fritz Todt, who ran it until his death in an air crash in February of the same year. The complex includes a number of personnel bunkers, FlaK emplacements, ammunition bunkers, etc. Note in the contemporary photo (**A**), taken after the battery fell, the stepped embrasure. This was intended to stop the mouth of the emplacement acting as a shot trap and reducing the likelihood of splinters or fragments penetrating the guncrew's fighting area.

A

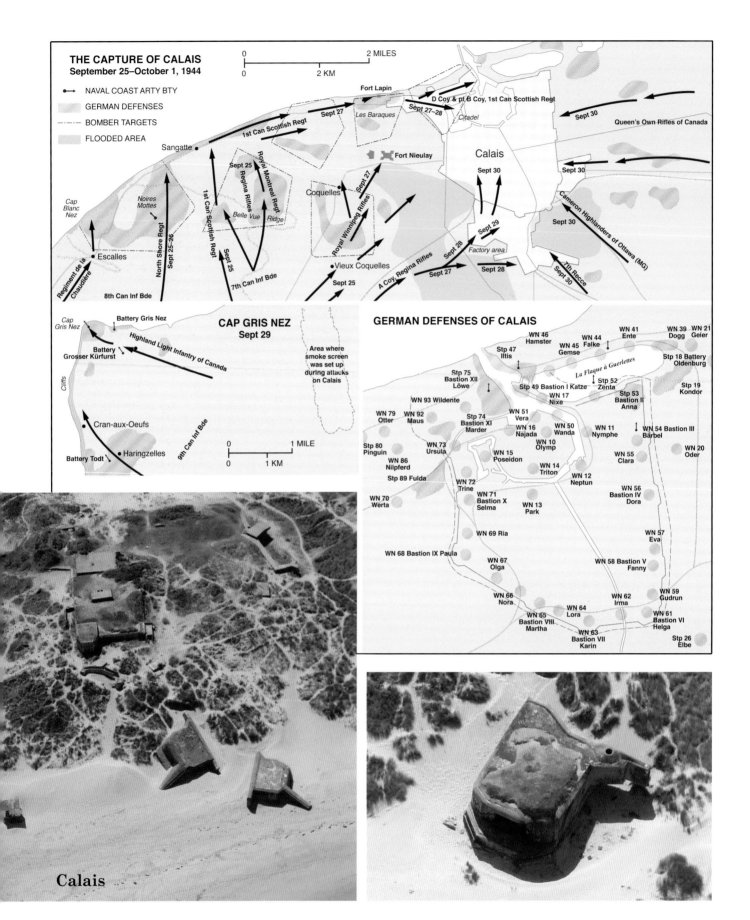

THE CAPTURE OF CALAIS
September 25–October 1, 1944

- NAVAL COAST ARTY BTY
- GERMAN DEFENSES
- BOMBER TARGETS
- FLOODED AREA

0 — 2 MILES
0 — 2 KM

Fort Lapin
D Coy & pt B Coy, 1st Can Scottish Regt
Sept 27
Les Baraques
Sept 27–28
Citadel
Queen's Own Rifles of Canada
1st Can Scottish Regt
Sangatte
Fort Nieulay
Calais
Sept 30
Sept 30
Sept 25
Royal Montreal Regt
Coquelles
Sept 27
Regina Rifles
Cameron Highlanders of Ottawa (MG)
Cap Blanc Nez
Noires Mottes
Belle Vue Ridge
Royal Winnipeg Rifles
Sept 29
Sept 30
1st Can Scottish Regt
Sept 25
Sept 30
Escalles
Sept 25
Sept 25–26
North Shore Regt
7th Can Inf Bde
Vieux Coquelles
Factory area
Sept 28
7th Recce
Regiment de la Chaudière
Sept 25
A Coy, Regina Rifles
Sept 27
Sept 28
Sept 30
8th Can Inf Bde

CAP GRIS NEZ
Sept 29

Cap Gris Nez
Battery Gris Nez
Highland Light Infantry of Canada
Area where smoke screen was set up during attacks on Calais
Battery Grosser Kürfurst
Cliffs
Cran-aux-Oeufs
Battery Todt
Haringzelles
9th Can Inf Bde

0 — 1 MILE
0 — 1 KM

GERMAN DEFENSES OF CALAIS

WN 41 Ente
WN 39 Dogg
WN 21 Geier
WN 46 Hamster
WN 44 Falke
Stp 47 Iltis
WN 45 Gemse
Stp 18 Battery Oldenburg
La Flaque à Guerlettes
Stp 75 Bastion XII Löwe
Stp 49 Bastion I Katze
Stp 52 Zenta
Stp 19 Kondor
WN 93 Wildente
WN 17 Nixe
Stp 53 Bastion II Anna
WN 79 Otter
WN 92 Maus
Stp 74 Bastion XI Marder
WN 51 Vera
WN 50 Wanda
WN 11 Nymphe
WN 54 Bastion III Bärbel
WN 16 Najada
Stp 80 Pinguin
WN 73 Ursula
WN 10 Olymp
WN 55 Clara
WN 20 Oder
WN 86 Nilpferd
WN 15 Poseidon
WN 14 Triton
Stp 89 Fulda
WN 12 Neptun
WN 56 Bastion IV Dora
WN 72 Trine
WN 70 Werta
WN 71 Bastion X Selma
WN 13 Park
WN 57 Eva
WN 69 Ria
WN 68 Bastion IX Paula
WN 67 Olga
WN 58 Bastion V Fanny
WN 66 Nora
WN 62 Irma
WN 59 Gudrun
WN 65 Bastion VIII Martha
WN 64 Lora
WN 61 Bastion VI Helga
WN 63 Bastion VII Karin
Stp 26 Elbe

Calais

Top: *Maps showing the course of Operation Undergo and the German strongpoints surrounding Calais.*

Above Left: *WN 79 ("Otter") is to the west of Fort Lapin. Sinking slowly into the sand are two R612 casemates; behind them a large command post which was tied in to the various batteries—Lindemann, Oldenburg, Todt, and Grosser Kurfürst—in the area.*

Above Right: *West of "Otter" is Stp Pinguin (penguin) only one of whose M176 casemates is visible. Behind this is Fort Lapin, originally a redoubt built in 1690. Over the years it was strengthened and between the wars it was rebuilt to house four 164.7mm guns. It formed part of the string of defenses around Calais (see also pp52–53).*

Opposite: *Calais from the air then and now.*

Battery Oldenburg

Above: *Stp 18, MKB Oldenburg, lies just east of Calais. As with the others in the chain that stretches to the Todt Battery south of Cap Gris Nez, construction of Oldenburg started in July 1940 when Operation Sea Lion, the invasion of England, was anticipated. The two open casemates (**A**, one shown **Below**) housed WWI-vintage Russian guns that Krupp had rechambered to 240mm. They could fire a 150kg projectile some 15 miles—short of the British coast but a danger to shipping. In 1942 the casemates were enclosed. On October 1, Oldenburg was taken by Canadian 3rd Inf Div.*

Above Right: *The interlocked defenses east of Calais near Le Fort Vert. At **B** the Oldenburg Battery; **C** Stp Waldam (also seen **Below Right**); **D** an R219 Doppelschartenstand (double gunports) part of WN Roland; **E** two R680s (casemate for 7.5cm PaK 40) of WN Rosamunde; **F** WN Ria—two R219s, an R612 Schartenstand für Lande-und Sturmabwehrgeschütz, and a 50mm KwK.*

Below Right: *Coastal battery M1 Waldam of Marine Artillery Section 244 had three 15cm SK C/28 guns in two M270 casemates and a unique revolving concrete cupola (SK Drehturm) which weighed 750 tons, installed on the rotating mechanism used to turn the main armament of the French battleship* Provence *(at **G**). Also shown are a command post (at **H**), a Lichtsprech bunker built to house equipment that used modulated light for communication (at **I**), and an R612 (at **J**).*

V-Weapons

The flying bomb campaign of 1944 was not just terrifying, sapping civilian morale, but did significant damage. 9,521 of the shorter-range V1s were fired at the UK June–October 1944, when the last site in range of Britain was overrun. Thereafter, they were directed at Antwerp and other targets in Belgium: 2,448 were launched up till March 29, 1945. The more deadly V2 was launched first against Paris on September 8, 1944, by Art. Abt. 444 Batterie from a position in Belgium. By war's end, nearly 3,200 others had followed, killing c. 9,000 civilians and military personnel mainly in London, Antwerp, and Liege.

Unlike the V1s, the V2s were fired by mobile launchers which were difficult to locate. As an example, Art. Abt. 836 Battalion (motorized), set up in September 1943, began launching rockets on Lille and Mons on September 14, 1944, from the Euskirchen area shortly after moving across the Rhine to the Westerwald area, north of Montabaur. It fired 432 rockets from here—mainly at Antwerp and Liege—until the deteriorating military situation led to the unit fighting as infantry from April 8, 1945. Constructing the V2s killed more than their warheads, most of the dead from forced labor in the Dora-Mittelbau concentration camps around Nordhausen. The factory produced some 4,575 V2s between August 1944 and March 1945. Of the 60,000+ detainees employed in and around the Mittelbau complex 1943–45, 26,500 did not survive.

A Test launch of a V2, developed by US space race guru Wernher von Braun.

B A crater caused by a V1 or V2 explosion, Fort de Merxim, Belgium, October 15,1944.

C Since the 1970s, the site of the former camp gate of Dora-Mittelbau has been marked by concrete pillars.

D Today it is hard to believe that this beautiful location in the Harz mountains could have been a concentration camp.

E Map showing the launching sites as identified in January 1944.

F A V1 flying bomb in flight.

G Death and destruction in Antwerp following a V2 strike.

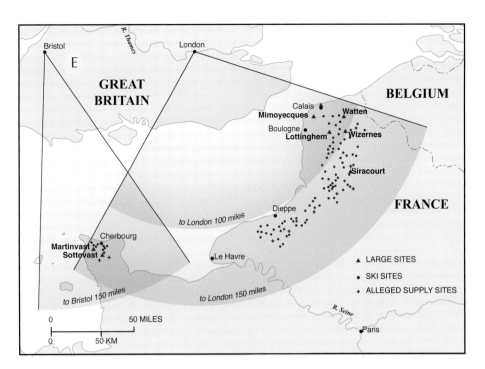

3 LIBERATING BELGIUM

Main photo: *Ostend had its fair share of defenses—including those identified here, part of Pz.Stp. Hafen that protected the harbor and locks:* **A** *Battery Hundius, with its M157 fire control post (***A2***, inset)and one of four R671 casemates (***A1***, inset, also visible on p58).* **B** *Halve Maan Battery, which had a number of emplacements for guns and FlaK.* **C** *An R633 bunker whose main armament was a 5cm M19 mortar. There's also a special transformer building that handled the town's electricity (***D***).*

Below: *Insignia of the Brigade Piron, the Belgian Group that fought from Belgium to Germany, mainly as part of British Second Army.*

Above: *West of the entrance to Ostend harbor lies Fort Napoleon (A) which was built in 1811. In both world wars it became the HQ for German artillery in the area. As outlined in the caption on p57, Ostend harbor was well defended. At B (also at A1 on p57) the most easterly casemate of Battery Hundius; this R671 would have housed a 10.5cm gun.*

Opposite: *The magnificent Domein Raversijde museum, just to the west of Ostend Airport. With well over 60 bunkers and batteries from both world wars, it was preserved by Prince Karel (1903–83), Count of Flanders and Regent of Belgium 1944–50, who lived here (house at F) from 1950. D is the entrance to the museum. Among the goodies on show are the WWI Aachen Battery (C); E is a WWI fire control post with a rangefinder in front. The WW2 battery was initially named MKB Saltzwedel neu but later called Tirpitz. G Various different anti-tank and anti-landing craft obstacles used on the beaches of the Atlantic Wall. H House used by battery commander. I (left, right, and detail photo below) two of the four R671 bunkers built. J WWII observation bunker and command post.*

The liberation of Belgium took two months—from September 2 when the 82nd Recon Bn of US 2nd Armd Div crossed the border at Rumes, southwest of Tournai, till November 3 when Canadian troops cleared the last German pocket in the northwest. The liberation had involved two army groups, the British–Canadian 21st and US 12th. The 21st Army Group consisted of the multinational Canadian First Army, commanded by Gen H.D.G. Crerar, tasked with taking the Channel ports and littoral, and British Second Army (Lt-Gen Miles Dempsey), which cleared most of central Belgium. The US 12th included US First Army (Gen Courtney Hodges), on the eastern side of the country and Patton's Third Army in France that only came into Belgium when events took a turn for the worse on December 16 when eastern Belgium was the location for the "Wacht am Rhein" counterattack. Belgium would only finally be free after this failed. (The Battle of the Bulge is dealt with in a separate chapter, pp118–155). The other US army in the 12th Army Group was the Ninth, which moved east after taking Brittany, arriving in October.

On the coast, Canadian 2nd Inf Division invested Dunkerque on September 6–17 and took Ostende without a fight on the 9th. The northwest corner, Zeebrugge, took longer to subdue, being part of the Scheldt clearing operation. It finally fell on November 1.

British Second Army liberated Brussels on September 3, Antwerp on the 4th, with help from the local resistance, and Ghent on the 6th. 4th Canadian Armoured moved toward Bruges, which was cleared on the 12th: luckily, the Germans left the beautiful city without a fight thus avoiding the destruction of what is today a Unesco World Heritage Site.

The US First Army crossed into Belgium on September 2 and drove east toward Aachen, liberating the region south of Brussels, reaching Liege on the 9th and Maastricht in Holland on September 14. Shortly after, First Army prepared to take Aachen, first attacking south, pushing into the Hürtgen Forest. Gone were the days of the *Rückmarsch*, and the German defense of the Hürtgen Forest was epic, lasting well into December. Casualties were high—First Army suffered over 29,000 dead and wounded. There was better news around Aachen, where after a similarly tough fight, the city fell on October 21.

After taking the French coast, the First Canadian Army entered Belgium. This Staghound of the XIIth Manitoba Dragoons is seen (**A**) at Blankenberghe on September 11, just before the unit took Bruges. This event—without any destruction of the fine medieval city—is remembered at the Canada bridge (**B**)—as the plaque on it says, "erected in memory of the Canadian forces who liberated the city of Bruges on September the 12th 1944." The two bison represent the XIIth Manitoba Dragoons (**C**). Collaborators were rounded up by the local population (**D**) and then the local sights were enjoyed (**E**).

Right and Below Right: *Maj. David Currie won the Victoria Cross at the battle of Falaise while serving with the South Alberta Regiment—the only Canadian VC for the Normandy campaign, and the only one awarded to a member of the Royal Canadian Armoured Corps. He's seen here (**Below Right**) in a Humber Mk I scout car in late 1944; note the Bren gun armament. The plaque is in downtown Owen Sound, Canada.*

Below: *Sweeping for mines at a roadblock, Kappellen, October 5.*

Bottom: *Canadian 4th Armd Div trained and fought alongside Polish 1st Armd at Falaise pocket and during the advance from Normandy. Involved in clearing the southern bank of the Scheldt, 4th Armd fought in the Breskens pocket, before being moved to the Netherlands.*

DAVID VIVIAN CURRIE. V.C. 1912-1986

A much-honoured World War II army officer, Currie, who is buried in Owen Sound, was born and raised in Saskatchewan. He enlisted in 1940 and was sent overseas with the 29th Canadian Armoured Reconnaissance Regiment (the South Alberta Regiment) three years later. On August 18, 1944, Currie, leading a small force in Normandy, was ordered to help seal the Chambois-Trun escape route to the German forces cut off in the Falaise pocket. He met fierce resistance in the village of St. Lambert-sur-Dives. There, by skilful command and heroic example, Currie sustained his men for three days as they repeatedly thwarted breakout attempts by masses of Germans. For his actions, he was awarded the Victoria Cross, the British Commonwealth's highest decoration for valour.

Erected by the Ontario Heritage Foundation,
Ministry of Culture and Communications

Having taken most of Belgium, the focus of the Allies' attack from mid-September concentrated on Operation Market Garden (see Chapter 4). After its failure, opening the Scheldt became of vital importance. The task was given to Canadian II Corps (which included Polish 1st Armd Div, British 49th and 52nd Divs, as well as British I Corps) and was accomplished between October 2 and November 8 (see Chapter 6).

Top: *The Canadian 3rd Inf Div encountered tenacious German resistance as it fought to cross the Leopold Canal.*

Above: *Much of low-lying Belgium and the Netherlands had been flooded which made movement and living difficult.*

Above Right: *Vehicles of Canadian 3rd Inf Div move through Bockhoute, October 8.*

Right: *The answer to the conditions were specialist vehicles, here a column of Alligator LVTs passing Terrapin amphibious vehicles on the Scheldt, October 13.*

Brigade Piron

The Belgian Brigade Piron was formed in 1943 and commanded by Lt-Col. Jean-Baptiste Piron (later Lt-Gen., DSO). In Normandy it was attached to 6th Airborne until August 26 when it came under command of the BR 49th Inf Div, later transferring to BR Second Army.

Left: Monument—with a Staghound turret—in memory of the soldiers of the Belgian Piron Brigade who fell during the liberation of Leopoldsburg and Heppen on September 11/12 when it fought with BR 8th Armd Div.

Below Left: Staghound Mk I Audemer in Brigade Piron colors is kept at the Tank Museum at Kappellen.

Bottom Left: The Belgian Film Unit followed Brigade Piron through occupied Europe.

Below: This monument to the 1st Belgian Brigade at Auberville in France talks of its role liberating "the villages of the Cote Fleurie from Sallenelles to Honfleur."

Bottom: Monument to Lt-Gen. J. Piron at Couvin near Namur.

Polish 1st Armored Division

Above: *Polish 1st Armd Div in Tielt, Belgium, against a backdrop still recognizable today.* **Inset** *is the Sherman Firefly presented to the city by the division.*

Right: *Lt. Kłaptocz of the 10th Dragoons, Polish 1st Armd Div, and Maj. Leonard Dull of the US 90th Inf Div, in Chambois, August 1944, after the Allied link-up closed the noose around the Falaise Pocket, trapping the remains of the German Seventh Armee. Kłaptocz later died fighting in Holland.*

Opposite:
A *Commander of Polish 1st Armd was General Stanisław Maczek (1892–1994). Treated shabbily by the British—who denied him a service pension after the war—and by the Communist government of his homeland until 1989, when Prime Minister Mieczysław Rakowski issued a public apology, in 1994 Maczek was presented with Poland's highest state decoration, the Order of the White Eagle. He is buried with his men in Breda (**B** see also page 157). Maczek also has a memorial (**C**) by Karin Hardonk in General Maczek Square, Stadskanaal, The Netherlands.*

*The Poles were welcomed in the Low Countries. St. Nicholas supplied them with a badge (**D**) and, later, Lt-Col. Aleksander Stefanowicz, Commander of 1st Polish Armd Regt, received the Regimental Colors (**E**) there on 3 March 1946. In Saint Omer a memorial (**F**) was erected to honor their liberators.*

S. W. MACZEK
GENERAŁ BRONI
DOWÓDCA 1.POL. DYW. PANC.

★ 31-3-1892
✝ 11-12-1994

65

Ghent

When the first British tanks rolled into the city, they received a tumultuous welcome. Armfuls of flowers were presented; beer and wine flowed. Gen. Gerald Verney, CO of 7th Armd Div, arrived in Ghent in a Staghound, on September 8 (**B, D, E**). He had taken over the division following Monty's reaction to the battle of Villers Bocage. The performance of British armor in general—and 7th Armd in particular—is debated to this day. Verney may have in public suggested that Monty felt the officers he moved should be given a chance to pass on their experience as trainers, or at least be relieved of the strain of active service conditions, elsewhere he said that the Desert Rats were "swollen-headed" and "deserved the criticism they received." This may have been true, but there are many issues that make this a rather simplistic view— the deficiencies of their new AFV, the Cromwell; the problems that all the Allies had when fighting offensively in the bocage; and the almost World War I levels of attrition for front-line units.

A Infantrymen of the King's Shropshire Light Infantry catch some sleep by the side of a 3RTR Sherman on the road to Ghent, exhausted by the speed of the advance.

C The Ghent Citation (left). It was presented to 5RTR in honor of their being the first regiment to enter Ghent. 7th Armd had advanced some 300 miles in around two weeks following the closing of the Falaise Pocket on August 21. Plaque (right) presented to the citizens of Ghent by the Desert Rats, made by the division's workshops.

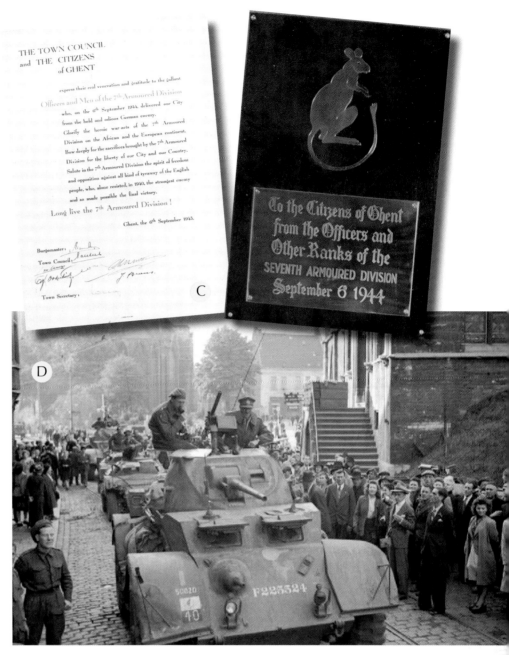

Brussels

A *Maj-Gen. "Pip" Roberts, commanding 11th Armd Div, in his White scout car, August 15.*

B *Shermans of the 23rd Hussars, 11th Armd Div, advance through Deurne, September 26. Note the "Charging Bull" on the first tank's front hull (third marking from the left), the division's emblem (also* **Inset***).*

*Liberation brought out the largest celebrations in Belgian history. British troops reached Brussels to a joyous reception (*C*, September 3.) *D *More British troops move into the center of the city (September 4). A carrier crewed by Free Belgian troops (*E*) is welcomed by cheering civilians.*

F *The crew of a Cromwell Mk IV tank of 2nd Welsh Guards on the drive into Brussels, September 3. Despite sporadic resistance from the Royal Palace and Gestapo HQ, the city's capture went smoothly, "the chief difficulty being to cope with the populace who were very effusive in their welcome," the battalion's war diary put it with typical understatement.*

US First Army

Originally commanded by Omar Bradley, the First Army was activated in Britain in January 1944. It played a significant role in the Normandy invasion, the breakout and pursuit, and when Bradley took over 12th Army Group, Courtney Hodges took over as CG. First Army was on the north of the Battle of the Bulge, took part in the battle of the Rhineland, and crossed the Rhine at Remagen. Reaching the Elbe on April 18 and meeting Soviet forces on the 25th, First Army ended the war in Europe and was earmarked for a role in Operation Downfall, the invasion of Japan, when the surrender ended that war.

As an example of the experience of the units of the First Army, the next few pages look at the 113th FA Bn, one of the organic units of 30th Inf Div, which came ashore on the continent of Europe June 10–15, 1944. The division joined First Army and acted as its spearhead from the St Lô breakout, through France and the Low Countries, into Germany. It held off the desperate German counterattack at Mortain, when 2nd Bn, 120th Inf Regt and 1st Bn, 117th Inf Regt, bore the brunt of the assault. Hard-pressed, all available personnel of the 30th Division were thrown into action. They held, broke the attack, and soon the enemy was thrown back.

Chasing the retreating Germans across France, the Seine River was soon crossed, and at the start of September, the division was the first Allied unit to enter both Belgium and the Netherlands. It helped take Tournai as part of the encirclement of the Mons pocket, advanced to the Meuse and liberated Maastricht before assaulting the Siegfried Line, and—with 1st Inf Div—encircling and taking Aachen, the first major German town to fall to the Allies. The thrust into Germany was halted when the Germans counterattacked in the Ardennes in December 1944. The 30th was rushed to the Malmedy–Stavelot–Stoumont area, which had been attacked by Jochen Peiper's 1st SS-Pz Div—the *Leibstandarte*, whom the 30th had met and beaten at Mortain. Again the 30th mauled some of Hitler's best troops, helping to stem the German winter drive, before moving to the Vielsalm–Sart–Lierneux areas, counterattacking and reaching St. Vith before being pulled out of combat to prepare for the battle of the Rhineland. 30th Division went on to record 282 days in combat 1944–1945, being assigned primarily to First Army as shown below.

DATE	CORPS	ARMY Assigned	ARMY Attached	ARMY GROUP Assigned	ARMY GROUP Attached
8 Feb '44		First		ETOUSA	
18 Feb	XIX	First			
15 Jul	VII	First		12th	
28 Jul	XIX	First		12th	
4 Aug	V	First		12th	
5 Aug	VII	First		12th	
13 Aug	XIX	First		12th	
26 Aug	XV	Third	First	12th	
29 Aug	XIX	First		12th	
22 Oct		Ninth		12th	
17 Dec	V	Ninth	First	12th	
21 Dec	XVIII AB	Ninth		12th	BR 21st
22 Dec	XVIII AB	First		12th	BR 21st
18 Jan '45	XVIII AB	First		12th	
3 Feb	XIX	Ninth		12th	
6 Mar	XVI	Ninth		12th	
30 Mar	XIX	Ninth		12th	
8 May	XIII	Ninth		12th	

XIX CORPS' DRIVE FROM THE ALBERT CANAL TO THE WESTWALL
September 10–19, 1944

- – – ··· Allied positions Sept 10
- ——▶ Main axis of advance with date
- ⊔⊔⊔ ○○○ Positions Sept 19 night
- ⊠ German unit
- ⬚ German line opposite XIX Corps, Sept 19
- △△△ Westwall

5   0   5   10 miles
5   0   5   10 km

Main photo: *American armor fans out near Gelin, Belgium.*

Left: *After taking part in the encirclement of German forces in the Mons pocket—remnants of a number of divisions who had retreated across France—the First Army attack stuttered due to the paucity of supplies. In spite of all the best efforts, they had outrun their logistics and 30th Division, as part of XIX Corps, waited for gasoline in Tournai, taking the opportunity to rest and to capture nearly 1,000 prisoners. When the gas arrived, XIX Corps advanced to the Albert Canal, taking Eben Emael—scene of the German airborne attack in 1940—and Maastricht, reaching the Westwall by mid-September. The battle for Aachen followed.*

Opposite: *Nicknamed the "Old Hickory" division, in honor of President Andrew Jackson, during WWII the 30th was one of the best—if not the best—of the Allied infantry divisions. Its shoulder patch is a combination of the letters "O" and "H" (for Old Hickory) and the Roman numeral for 30 (XXX).*

The 113th Field Artillery Battalion was one of four divisional artillery battalions and consisted of 12 x 155mm howitzers which could fire a 95lb projectile about 14,000 yards. The late Dr. Van Heely was Battalion Assistant S3 in the 113th Field Artillery. Dr. Heely told Mike Williard the following story concerning the collection of photos on the 30th Division's website:

"When the 113th was at Aschersleben after the war, they found a bombed out Ju88 aircraft manufacturing plant with a complete photography lab. Dr. Van Heely collected undeveloped film from across the battalion and developed it at the plant. Everyone that donated film to the effort was given a complete set of prints."

Above Left: Heely's caption —
" 'Gopher Heely' When the shells whistled, I'd 'gopher' that hole in a helluva hurry."
Mortain, France August 1944.

Left and Below Left: German Panthers knocked out during Operation Lüttich at Mortain, August 1944.

Below: The unit lost its first men on the voyage to Omaha Beach on June 15, when LST #133 hit a mine. The after action report identified 2 men killed, 8 injured, and 20 missing, 18 of whom are recorded on the wall of the missing at the Normandy American Cemetery.

Above: *The coat of arms was originally approved for the 113th FA* Regiment *on February 24, 1931. It was redesignated for the 113th FA* Battalion *on July 29, 1942.*

Above Right: *113th FA Bn officers at St. Romphaire, France, August 1944.* Left to Right: First Row; *Capt. Harold Horner, Maj. S. L. McCall, Lt. Wade S. Kolb, Lt. Edward L. McMullen, Capt. Abbott C. Weatherly, Capt. Howard L. Krall, Capt. Van K. Heely, Lt. Walter J. Horan, Lt. R.H. Bradley.*
Second Row; *Capt. William B. Carlton, Lt. George P. Eldridge, Capt. George R. Springer, Capt. Hyman M. Bizzell, Capt. Clement T. Ziegler, Lt. Marvin L. Woodruff, Lt. Elmer G. Rosenberger, Lt. Russell D. Stewart, Lt. Harold E. Hunt, Maj. Wiley C. Rodman.*
Third Row; *Lt. Adrian A. VanHook, Lt. Bulla ??, Lt. ??, Lt. ??, Capt. Robbins ??, Capt. Wendell A. Roberts, Capt. Bernard J. Levy, Lt. William R. Fuller, WOJG Howard S. Maney, Lt. Norman G. Stroud.*
Not present at time of photo; *Lt.Col. Edward F. Griffin, Capt. Richard J. Binnicker, Lt. Paul E. Griffin, Lt. Bob Spicer, Lt. Robert C. Anderson, WOJG Astor C. Lucas.*

Center Right and Right: *Passing through Tongeren (**Center**) and another Belgian town in September, during the headlong pursuit of the retreating Germans.*

Above Left and Above: *Fort Eben Emael, in September 1944 and today. This is the main entrance protected by an anti-tank gun and machine gun positions.*

Center and Below Left: *XIX Corps engineers performed miracles around the area of Maastricht where all the bridges across the canal and river had been destroyed. 234th ECB crossed the river south of Vise with treadways before moving up the east bank of the river with 30th Division to build a bridge to Maastricht—all of which was accomplished on the same day, September 14. Here (**Center**) a destroyed bridge over the Meuse at Vise, south of Maastricht and (**Below**) the pontoon bridge across the Albert Canal put up by 234th ECB.*

Above Right and Right: *113th FA Bn crossing the Meuse River south of Vise.*

Below Right: *V1 "buzz bomb" in flight, December 1944. The forerunner of the cruise missile was incapable of a surgical strike, but proved an effective terror weapon— and one that saw the strategic bombing campaign diverted from bombing German means of production to strike at the launching sites. The first V1 was launched against London on June 13, 1944. This was followed by a salvo of 244 fired from 55 sites in northern France late the next day. Flakgruppe Creil would launch around a hundred a day from then on. As June drew to a close, the civilian death toll had reached 1,800. Operation Crossbow—the use of strategic bombers—and the Allied advance after Operation Cobra destroyed the French launching sites but Flakgruppe Creil redeployed and in late October the bombs started raining down on Brussels. 55 were launched and then, five days later, Antwerp became the Germans' main target, with others aimed at Charleroi and Liege. Over 750 were fired by the end of November. By the time the Canadians overran the launching sites in north Holland, nearly 6,000 flying bombs had fallen within eight miles of the center of Antwerp, killing 2,423 and sinking over 50 ships and barges in the port restricting its operation. (See also pp54–55.)*

Martin Blumenson—the well-respected biographer of Patton—wrote the *Breakout and Pursuit* volume of the official history of the war (the so-called "Green Books"). Of this period he says, "Though it was not to become obvious for a week or so, the Allied troops were tired. The pursuit had been wearing on men and equipment. Casualties had not been heavy at any one place, but their cumulative effect reduced the strength of all combat units. Tanks and vehicles had gone so long and so far without proper maintenance and repair that in one armored division less than a third of the authorized number of medium tanks were actually fit for combat. Another had had so many tanks fall out of column because of mechanical failure or lack of gasoline that its equipment was spread over the countryside between Valenciennes and Luxembourg, more than a hundred miles. Since the gasoline shortage prevented transferring vehicles for repair, mobile crews performed on-the-spot adjustments when they were able, but those tanks that needed shop treatment had long to wait." Added to this was the belief that the enemy was on the run and close to being finished. But as the Allies were soon to find out, this was far from the case: Patton was about to confront Metz; the First Army to do battle in the Hürtgen Forest; and in the Netherlands, the Allies were about go for the "Bridge Too Far" and all this was going to take place in a wet European autumn.

A *This monument, in honor of the soldiers of the "Old Hickory," is placed on the spot where the division crossed the Maas and liberated the city of Maastricht. It was dedicated on September 14, 1994, commemorating the 50th anniversary of the liberation.*

B *The actual crossing.*

C *American infantry pass the Maastricht city limits sign.*

D *Germans captured in Maastricht.*

E *The main square in Maastricht, the Vrijthof, is where one can find (**F and inset**) the bronze medallion presented to the city by 30th Division Association.*

For more about 30th Division see pp128–129 in Chapter 5.

CHAPTER 4
OPERATION MARKET GARDEN

The US 82nd AB Div, under Brig-Gen. James M. Gavin, dropped northeast of the 101st Div to take the bridges at Grave and Nijmegen. In the 82nd AB Div, 89% of troops landed on or within 1,000 meters (3,300 ft) of their drop zones and 84% of gliders landed on or within 1,000 meters (3,300 ft) of their landing zones—a substantial improvement on the June 5/6 drop. After the Battle's excellent two-volume coverage of the operation starts with a quote from Gavin:

"We knew the risks were great, but we believed that the battle we were about to fight would bring the war to an end."

Above: *Gen. Lewis H. Brereton (left) had been made commander of the First Allied Airborne Army on its creation in early August 1944. Here he is talking to the CO of 434th Troop Carrier Group, who will fly the lead 101st Airborne aircraft. The other man is CO of the 327th GIR, Col. Joseph Harper.*

Opposite, Below: *The modern "bridge too far" at Arnhem—the John Frost Bridge is named after the CO of the British forces who reached it.*

Below: *Getting to the start line meant taking the Albert and Meuse-Escaut canal bridges. XXX Corps did this in early September, but the opposition was fierce and showed that German resistance had stiffened after the rout. Here troops cross the Escaut on September 19.*

Operation Market Garden is another strongly debated subject among WW2 historians: was it a brave attempt to end the war early that foundered for being a bridge too far or was it, rather, an ill-conceived waste of resources that should have been used on another front? With hindsight, there's no doubt that the operation was a daring —if not risky—attempt to attack deep into enemy territory proposed by a general often disparaged for being too conservative. But at the beginning of September, it seemed to the Allied commanders that the enemy was disorganized; it had lost many men, huge numbers of vehicles, and had retreated helter-skelter through France and Belgium. In reality, the Germans had already started a brilliant fire brigade reorganization and would soon have an effective defense throughout the Netherlands. With von Rundstedt returning to take over as OB West, Generalfeldmarschall Walter Model—Hitler's fireman, to use the well-known soubriquet— concentrated on rebuilding Armeegruppe B. In this task he was helped by the appointment of Generaloberst Kurt Student as commander of First Fallschirmjäger Armee—initially a paper army, it would prove a thorn in the Allies' side throughout the campaign in the Low Countries—and the arrival of new units. As an example of this, take the arrival of 107th Pz Bde in theater. Formed in Poland based on what remained of 25th PzGr Div, it had six weeks to train and receive its equipment: between August 14 and September 1 it received 154 SdKfz 251s, 36 Panther Gs, and 11 Jagdpanzer IV L/70s. Commanded by Lt-Col. Berndt-Joachim Freiherr von Maltzahn, it traveled west by 15 trains to Venlo between September 16–18, ordered to help defend the Westwall near Aachen. Maltzahn arrived on the evening of the 17th and was immediately instructed to use what forces he had at his disposal to attack the 101st Airborne at Son.

While there is an element of the fortuitous about this, Operation Market Garden did not came unstuck because of bad luck, although bad weather (which both Eisenhower and Montgomery cited as a significant factor) played a part. As Bob Kershaw's excellent *It Never Snows in September* identifies, Allied historians are quick to identify mistakes, rather than examine the remarkable German achievement. The real reason the operation failed was that the Germans were able to flood reinforcements into the area faster than the Allies and enough of them were combat-experienced to ensure that the younger greenhorns alongside them stuck to their task. As in the east, the Germans showed a remarkable ability to improvise an effective defense when their attackers seemed to have the upper hand. But it was a close-run thing.

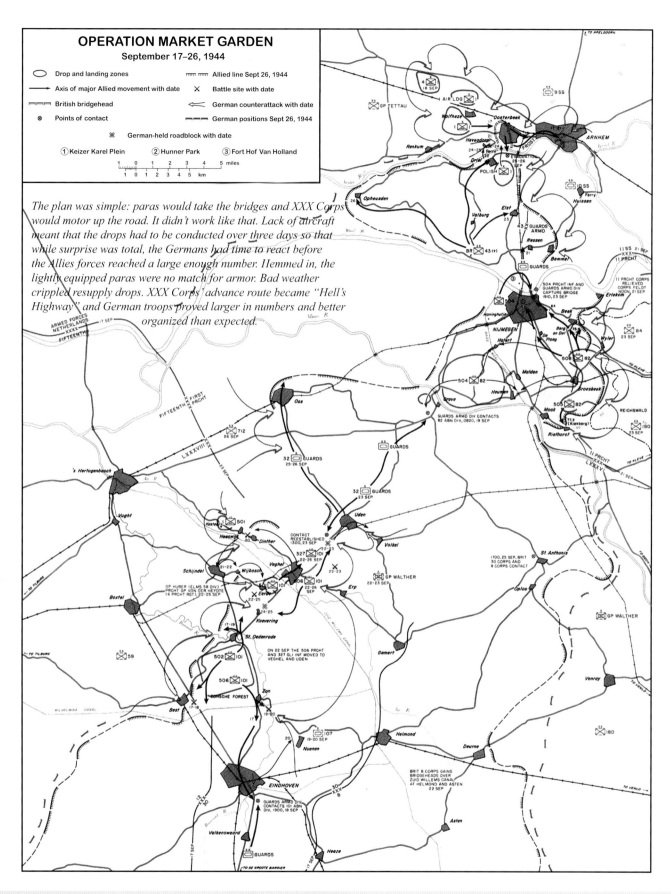

OPERATION MARKET GARDEN
September 17–26, 1944

⬭ Drop and landing zones	⊪⊪⊪ Allied line Sept 26, 1944
→ Axis of major Allied movement with date	✕ Battle site with date
⌓⌓⌓ British bridgehead	⟵ German counterattack with date
⊗ Points of contact	‐‐‐ German positions Sept 26, 1944
✕ German-held roadblock with date	

① Keizer Karel Plein   ② Hunner Park   ③ Fort Hof Van Holland

1 0 1 2 3 4 5 miles
1 0 1 2 3 4 5 km

The plan was simple: paras would take the bridges and XXX Corps would motor up the road. It didn't work like that. Lack of aircraft meant that the drops had to be conducted over three days so that while surprise was total, the Germans had time to react before the Allies forces reached a large enough number. Hemmed in, the lightly equipped paras were no match for armor. Bad weather crippled resupply drops. XXX Corps' advance route became "Hell's Highway" and German troops proved larger in numbers and better organized than expected.

101st Airborne

Above: *1st Bn, 501st PIR, on its way. Leading the 45-aircraft formation is Col. Whitacre, the 434th Group commander. This photo was taken from the astrodome of his C-47.*

Right: *Most of 501st PIR dropped outside Veghel on DZ "A" and by 15:00 had already taken the four bridges that were the initial objectives. By nightfall the regiment was set to defend the town against enemy attack. The 502nd PIR landed on DZ "B" and seized St. Oedenrode and the bridge over the Dommel. Part of the 3rd Bn took the road bridge at Best, but was forced away by a strong counterattack. 506th PIR landed on DZ "C." After making their way to the three bridges over the Wilhelmina Canal outside Son, they discovered all of them had been blown up. This made the bridge at Best crucial and the battle to take it raged.*

Opposite, Above: *This dramatic shot shows the result of a midair collision between two Wacos.*

Opposite, Below: *This doctor's house in Veghel acted as HQ for 501st PIR. In its grounds (Inset right) is the Kangaroo monument (Kangaroo was the callsign of 101st Airborne).*

Opposite, Inset left: *Memorial in Best to Lt-Col. Robert G. Cole who won the Medal of Honor at Carentan. He was killed in action on September 18, 1944, and is buried at the American Cemetery in Margraten.*

Opposite, Inset center: *Memorial to 101st Airborne at Son.*

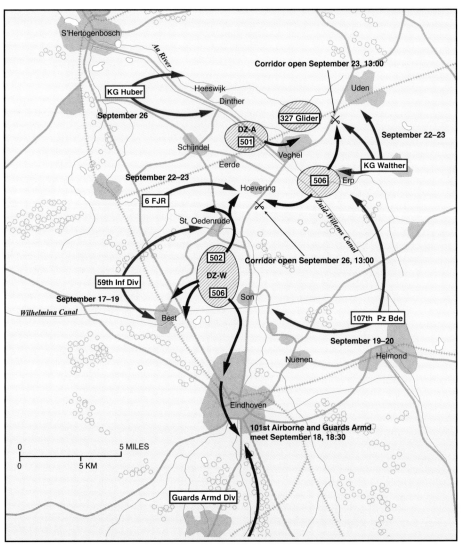

A *Son Bridge today. The Liberation Route starts in Normandy and continues via Nijmegen and Arnhem in the direction of Berlin. There are 82 boulders at various locations throughout the region; this one (A1) is at Son Bridge.*

B *14th Field Sqn, RE replaced Son Bridge overnight on September 18/19 allowing the Grenadier Guards to rush toward Grave, 36 hours behind schedule.*

C *Dutch farmers Driek Eykemans and Toon Wervoort give the glider men a lift. The pipe smoker is Japp Bothe one of the five Dutch Commandos of No. 2 (Dutch) Troop of No. 10 (Inter Allied) Cdo attached to 101st. Veghel, September 18.*

D *In Eindhoven the 101st was held up by two German 88s at the Kloosterdreel-Woenselsestraat intersection. One was destroyed by 506th PIR; this one was spiked by its crew before surrendering. XXX Corps vanguard reached Eindhoven at midday on the 18th.*

E *September 20, a Sherman of A Sqn 44RTR in Son. In front, German PoWs take a Wehrmacht handcart to the PoW compound.*

F *The Parachutist at Son. The panel reads:*

"Liberated on September 17, 1944, by the 506th PIR and elements of the 326th Airborne Engineers. This town was the

command post of the 101st Airborne Division during the first three days of the Holland campaign. The 506th Parachute Field Artillery, and the 81st Airborne AA Battalion, successfully repulsed all attacks on this position from D-Day to D+3 thereby enabling Div HQ to establish the command function so necessary to the success of the overall mission ..."

G *In memory of Joe Mann, 502nd PIR, who won the Medal of Honor on September 9 at Best when a grenade*

"landed within a few feet ... Unable to raise his arms, which were bandaged to his body, he yelled 'grenade' and threw his body over the grenade."

Right: and Below Right *This sequence of photos is officially dated the 23rd, but After The Battle—the yardstick for any researcher—suggests it is more likely to be the Skytrain of 1Lt. Jesse M. Harrison of the 435th Group which crashed on the 19th, during the second wave of drops.*

Bottom Right: *Gen. McAuliffe gives the second-wave crews and pilots a motivational speech. Commander of 101st Airborne divisional artillery, McAuliffe became assistant division commander when Don Pratt died on June 6, 1944. He is best remembered for the response "Nuts," to the suggestion that the encircled defenders of Bastogne should surrender.*

Opposite:

A *Having taken Eindhoven and made contact with XXX Corps, on the 19th 101st Airborne's task was to keep the corridor open. It did so in face of constant attacks, including those by the newly arrived 107th Pz Bde around Son. On the 19th the 502nd PIR took the bridge at Best, knocking out a number of 88s, killing 300, and taking over 1,000 captives. Here a British XXX Corps truck explodes after being hit by a 107th Pz Brigade shell or mortar bomb on Hell's Highway near Son on September 20. Movement along Hell's Highway stopped after this explosion and trucks were stacked up on the road from Son to the Belgium border.*

B *Shermans of 44RTR lined up in the village of Veghel on September 21. 44RTR supported the 101st Airborne in the battle to retain control of Hell's Highway. There was continued heavy fighting around Veghel, Eerde, and St Oedenrode, with the highway being cut on the 24th and rejoined on the 25th/26th.*

C *101st Airborne paratroopers move past a burning truck in Veghel on September 23. The battles along Hell's Highway continued to cause problems for reinforcements.*

D *British trucks from XXX Corps begin moving again on September 25. The German attacks at Eerde and Koevering on the 24th had temporarily cut the road and allowed German tanks to shoot up truck columns. The ones pushed into the ditch included 30 lorries from 536th Coy, RASC and a number filled with returning glider pilots of the 313th Troop Carrier Group, most of whom were lucky to escape.*

E *A Coy, 1st Bn, 501st PIR fought a bloody battle at Eerde, southwest of Veghel. Here they are showing some trophies.*

F *A 44RTR Sherman knocked out on September 25, near Koevering, in support of 506th PIR by a German Jagdpanther.*

A

82nd Airborne Division

C

B

D

Right: *82nd Airborne, under Brig-Gen. James M. Gavin, dropped northeast of the 101st to take the bridges at Grave (over the Meuse) and Nijmegen (over the Waal). The accuracy of the drop at Grave was good, landing only 600 yards to the southwest and the bridge fell quickly to the platoon of Lt. John S. Thompson from E Coy, 504th PIR. The 82nd would defend it against repeated attacks. However, the vital Nijmegen Bridge was still in German hands. Lead elements of XXX Corps—in the form of the Household Cavalry—reached Grave Bridge at 08:30 on the 19th, having made good time from Son, but Nijmegen bridge did not fall until 18:30 on the 20th. This delay proved critical to the whole operation.*

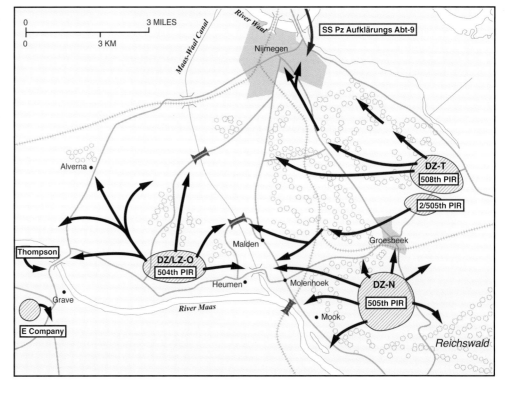

A *82nd Airborne memorial close to Grave bridge.*

B *Casemate South—one of the two bunkers defending the south side of the bridge. The two opened as a museum in 2011.*

C and D *The bridge over the Maass at Grave was named for Lt. John S. Thompson in 2004.*

E *A couple of miles away there's another memorial to the 82nd at a landing fields.*

Above: *XXX Corps was faced with a logistical nightmare. Over 20,000 vehicles had to move 64 miles in three days. The two lanes of a road often flanked by ditches made it easily blocked and ideal for delaying actions. Added to this, the throng of Dutch well-wishers slowed the column down in the larger towns. However, in spite of the problems at Son Bridge, the heroic efforts of 101st Airborne at Veghel and the 82nd at Grave, meant that by 10:00 on the 19th, the Grenadier Guards were in Nijmegen—behind schedule, but now only 10–12 miles from Arnhem.*

194661

195702

A *Brig-Gen. James Gavin, CG 82nd Airborne, puts on his main parachute. Note the M1 Garand rifle and his gear in front of him.*

B *Gavin's stick on board. Left is Col. John Norton, the Division G-3 (Operations Officer); next to him Capt. Hugo Olson, Gavin's aide. Both men carry SCR-536 walkie-talkie radios for communication after the jump.*

C *A last-minute briefing. Note 82nd Airborne cloth badge on the officer's left shoulder, his M1 Garand rifle and the mass of personal equipment—entrenching tool etc.*

D *Frame from a cine film of the drop by the 505th PIR. The lighter-colored chutes are supply containers.*

E *Coy C 307th Airborne Engr Bn dropped on DZ "N" at Groesbeek.*

F *49 of the 50 Waco gliders sent on D-Day reached the Netherlands. Landing in the soft fields was a hazard as shown here. The gliders were used to bring in heavier weapons in the form of Bty A, 80th AB AA/ATk Bn (jeep-towed 57mm ATk guns) and the Armd Recon Pl (four armored jeeps). The Wacos also carried Div Arty HQ, USAAF Air Support Signal Team, a British Phantom team, and nine Dutch commandos.*

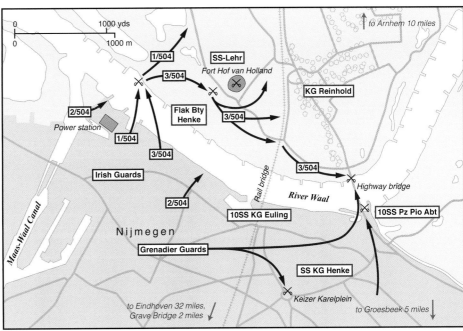

A *Today there are three bridges over the Waal at Nijmegen:* 1 *is the most recently built and runs across the area stormed by the assault river crossing of the 504th at around 15:00 on September 20.* 2 *is the Hot Van Holland strongpoint, set in a moated 19th century fort.* 3 *is the railway bridge, the north end of which the 504th took at 17:00.* 4 *is the road bridge. At 16:30 the paratroops had it under fire when a troop of tanks from 2nd Grenadier Guards crossed over. Two were knocked out. One great surprise was that the bridge wasn't blown by the Germans. The commander of the defense—Brigadeführer Heinz Harmel—had prepared it for demolition but Model wanted it intact for a counterattack. When Harmel did order it blown, the charges failed to detonate. Exactly why this happened is open to conjecture, but many believe it was down to a young Dutch student, Jan van Hoof, who cut the cables on Monday, September 18. He was killed on the 19th, so the story died with him, but he is honored for his role by a stone relief (B) on the bridge.*

C *Shows the memorial to those who died on the crossing—48 men although there are 49 names on the stone, including in error Gerald Page Hereford who died elsewhere—on the north bank of the Waal (although it was moved while the new bridge was constructed).*

D *On the 70th anniversary of "Market Garden" this Waco glider airframe replica was unveiled at "Little Amerika" in Groesbeek.*

E *Nijmegen's Grote Markt and St. Steven's church with the spans of the railway bridge (5) behind.* 6 *is roughly where the assault crossing set off, near the power station chimneys.*

Nijmegen was not where Operation Market Garden was lost, but it was where the failure became apparent. First, the bridge over the Waal wasn't taken quickly enough. 82nd Airborne—whose third lift of nearly half its gliders wouldn't arrive until the 23rd—concentrated on securing the strategic Groesbeek Heights allowing the Germans to set up a more effective defense of the bridge, with the 10th SS-Pz Div's Kampfgruppe Reinhold arriving on September 18. XXX Corps arrived on the 19th but it took a hard fight—including the incredible bravery of 3/504th PIR in an almost suicidal assault across the Waal in canvas boats—and a tank attack by Guards Armoured to take the bridge. 1st Troop, 1 Sqn, 2nd Grenadier Guards rushed across at dusk—a Firefly and three Sherman 75mms. Two of the Shermans were knocked out, the others pressed on reaching the railway viaduct about half a mile further on where they met up with the 504th PIR. The next tank across was Capt. Lord Peter Carrington's. Engaged by a Panzerfaust at the north end of the bridge, he waited to guard the access until the infantry arrived. Once it did, he went on to the viaduct. There, much to the annoyance of the 82nd Airborne paras, the tanks waited for dawn and infantry to arrive to assist the advance. In doing so—understandable though that pause may have been with the enemy still in the area and the flat countryside ahead—they lost the opportunity to break through to Arnhem. They could not know how few forces lay between them and their goal. By the time they did attack the Germans had gathered sufficient forces to block their advance ... and the British Paras at Arnhem Bridge had surrendered.

Whether an immediate attack could have fought and won through to Arnhem—and whether it would have been in sufficient numbers to achieve anything when it got there—is, of course, conjecture.

Above Left and Above: *17pdr anti-tank gun of the 21st Anti-Tank Regt, Guards Armd Div, guards the approaches to Nijmegen Bridge, seen with a cycletrack today.*

Below and Left: *Then and now views of the road bridge at Nijmegen. As the Guards moved off, on Groesbeek Heights, the 82nd were coping with a major counterattack by a Fallschirmjäger Kampfgruppe. It was broken up at Mook with the help of tanks from 3 Sqn Coldstream Guards. At Beek, it was also touch and go as the 508th PIR was pushed out of its positions: they regained them on the 21st, again with tank support. The 82nd would continue fighting on the heights until the night of September 30/ October 1.*

1st Airborne Division

The British and Polish landings at Arnhem, the subsequent battle, and the loss of some 8,000 men (nearly 1,500 killed; around 6,500 captured or missing) was a significant reverse for the Allies that condemned the Netherlands to the awful "Hunger Winter," and failed to deliver its strategic goal of bypassing the Westwall. Faulty intelligence, a significant underestimation of the German troops in the area (see map p98), bad weather—all contributed to the British failure to hold Arnhem.

Above Left: This vertical view of LZ "Z" has been reoriented to a similar angle as shown at **3** in the "now" image below. Taken on the 17th it shows Horsa and Hamilcar gliders of the 1st Airlanding Brigade.

Center Left: Men of 1st Bn, 1st Para Bde arriving on LZ "Z."

Above: It's a long way from the landing grounds to the bridge— some 6–7 miles along the quickest route **1** Arnhem bridge. **2** Oosterbeek. **3** The Hartenstein Hotel. The routes taken are shown on the map on p102. **4 and detail** Just visible is the Airborne Memorial.

Left: Key shows landing areas on September 17. **1** DZ "X"/LZ "X"; **2 and 3** LZ "Z"; **4** DZ "Y" at Ginkel Heath; **5** LZ "S"; **6** Wolheze; **7** today's A50 motorway; **8** toward Oosterbeek.

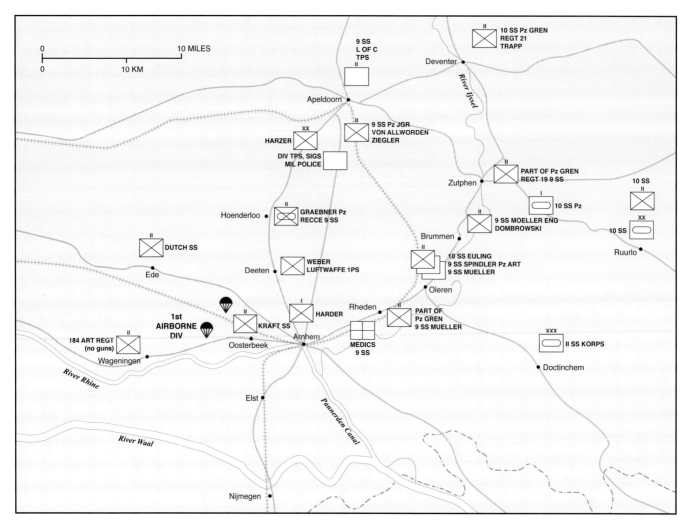

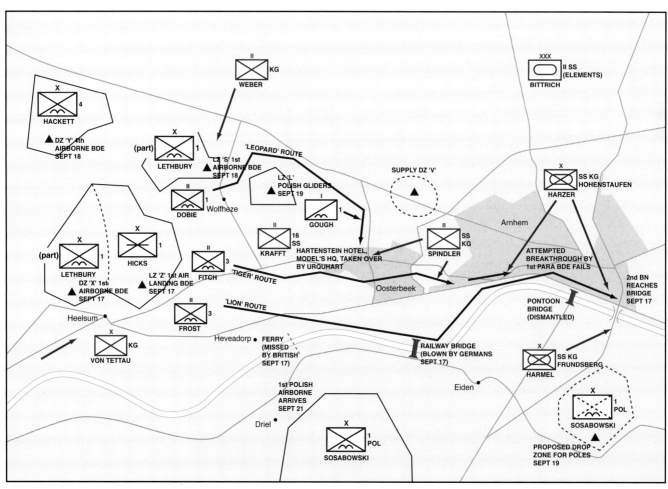

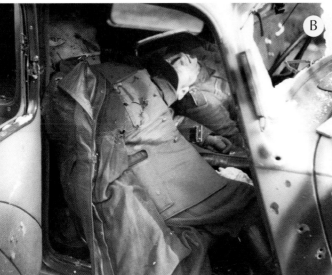

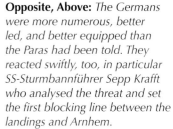

Opposite, Above: *The Germans were more numerous, better led, and better equipped than the Paras had been told. They reacted swiftly, too, in particular SS-Sturmbannführer Sepp Krafft who analysed the threat and set the first blocking line between the landings and Arnhem.*

Opposite, Below: *The landing areas, the planned routes into Arnhem, and the initial German response. On the 17th only Lt-Col. John Frost, and his 2nd Bn reached the bridge (see p101).*

This Page: *September 18, and the fighting had intensified. Frost is penned in at the bridge; the landing fields are under pressure; the 1st and 3rd Bns are finding progress into Arnhem slow and costly.*
A *Guarded by glider pilots, these Waffen-SS soldiers were part of Krafft's unit.*
B *and* **C** *Generalmajor Friedrich Kussin—commander of the Military HQ for the Arnhem area—died when his car was fired on by men from B Coy, 3rd Bn. He had just been to see Krafft in Wolfheze and was returning to his HQ.*
D *Brig. "Pip" Hicks, CO 1st Airlanding Bde, took over temporary command of the division in the absence of Gen. Roy Urquhart and Brig. G. Lathbury who had got caught up in the fighting.*
E *Men of the Recce Sqn near Wolfheze railway station.*

A

Above, Opposite, and Top:
Then and now views of Arnhem Bridge—from 1977 named the John Frost Bridge after the commander of the British troops. Today's bridge is a modern replica, completed in 1948, the original having been bombed in October 1944. The then image was taken after the battle—note the pillbox at right (A), scene of a sharp battle on the 17th.

Above Right: *Taken in 1945 from the east of Arnhem this Panzer Mk IV has been knocked out by the defenders of the Arnhem bridge. The twin towers of the St. Walburgis Basilica can be seen in the background.*

Right: *This photo of the bridge on the 18th shows the wreckage of the 9th SS Recce Bn column returning from Nijmegen. It tried to dash across the bridge and was destroyed in the process: some 70 Germans were killed.*

Lt-Col. John Frost, CO of 2nd Bn, the Parachute Regiment, left his dropping zone in the early afternoon of the 17th and moved toward the Arnhem road bridge using the southern route, codenamed "Lion." Most of 2nd Para Bn and a number of other supporting units—including four 6-pdr anti-tank guns, Brigade HQ, and Royal Engineers (some 740 men)—reached the center of Arnhem as night fell. They were able to secure the undefended northern end of the road bridge and Lt. Jack Grayburn, commanding A Coy's No 2 Pl, attempted to cross the bridge and take the southern end. The attack was halted by a pillbox (see **A** at photo opposite) but was unsuccessful, as was a later attempt using a flamethrower.

 The British troops dug in and were able to fight off an attack by 10th SS Recce Bn and other German units. The next day, September 18, at around 09:00, the 9th SS-Pz Div Hohenstaufen's Recce Bn returned from Nijmegen and tried to cross the bridge. It was stopped with heavy losses—including commanding officer Hauptsturmführer Viktor Gräbner—in a two-hour battle. Frost and the Paras expected other Airborne forces to join them from Oosterbeek, but each attempt was beaten back. They expected to be relieved by XXX Corps after three days: they held their positions until they ran out of ammunition and were captured on September 21.

E

F

A The closest 1st and 3rd Bns got to linking with Frost at the bridge was on the 19th in an early morning attack. This German photo shows the SS-Panzergrenadiers who had just fought them off.

B The assault guns of Sturmgeschütz-Brigade 280 played a significant role in halting the British advancing into Arnhem. Like 107th Panzer it was on its way to Aachen by train and was stopped en route. The StuGs and infantry of Kampfgruppe Molle advance.

C German infantry wait to follow the StuGs into the attack.

D After the Oosterbeek hospitals were overrun, the Germans moved the wounded out. This shows Capt Robson being helped out past a StuG IIIG.

E Seen on the 24th during fighting around the Oosterbeek pocket, this Sturmhaubitze 42G has a short 10.5cm howitzer. It's passing under the parachute from a supply drop.

F The StuGs arrived in Arnhem on the 19th. The StuG of the CO of 3 Batterie (in helmet) Oberwachtmeister Josef Mathes seen that day.

Opposite: *The bridge and surrounding area today. There are a number of memorials to the battle, including at **A** a Canadian 25pdr in the Jacobus Groenewoud Plantsoen—named after a reserve captain of the Infantry, the only Dutch officer killed during the fighting for the bridge, who was posthumously awarded with the Militairy Willemsorde. The Canadians liberated Arnhem in April 1945. On this gun is a plaque to 16 Parachute Field Ambulance (RAMC), one of the medical units with Frost. At **B** in the center of Airborneplein roundabout—also known as the Bear-pit—is the Airborne Memorial, comprising a column from the otherwise destroyed prewar Palace of Justice.*

Left and Below: *The area that Frost's force held September 17–21.*

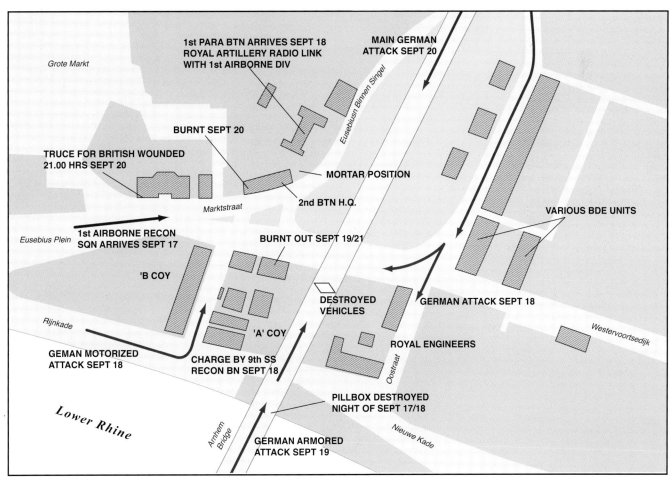

Polish 1st Independent Para Brigade

The 1st Polish Independent Para Bde landed south of the river on September 21, delivered there—as had been the British Paras on previous days—by US TCC. The weather was poor in the UK leading to the cancellation of much of their fighter cover, but the US aircrew performed with great bravery particularly when their low altitude led to heavy flak—33 of the 72 were damaged in all, five were destroyed. Of the c. 1,500 Poles that set off, just over 1,000 reached the landing grounds. The biggest problem for the Poles once on the ground was that the Driel ferry had been put out of action and the crossing was menaced by enemy on the high ground across the river. There were no obvious means to get across to the Oosterbeek perimeter, but nevertheless a number crossed, but without suitable boats insufficient to alter the outcome of the battle, and so the last chance to reinforce the bridgehead was lost. In the end 92 men of the brigade died at Arnhem and 111 were captured or missing.

Above: A monument raised to the Polish commander, Maj-Gen. Stanislav Sosabowski ("a Great Polish Hero") by the British 1st Airborne Division, 2006.

Above Right: As the weather improved, on the 23rd the third lift of US gliders (408 for the 82nd; 84 for the 101st) took place as did the second attempt to drop those members of the Polish Para Bde who hadn't got off on the 21st (41 aircraft). The latter were dropped at Grave and made their way to Driel overland. Note the Wacos on the ground: the 82nd glider drop was still in progress when the Polish drop took place.

Right: The Polish monument at Driel. was placed in the "Polenplein" (Polish Square) in the 1960s. The plaque on the wall at right is a memorial to the 5th Battalion Duke of Cornwall's Light Infantry part of 43rd (Wessex) Div.

The Oosterbeek Perimeter

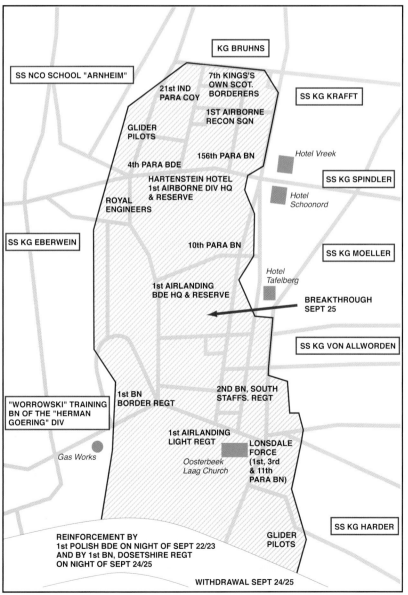

Top: *An abandoned vehicle outside Oosterbeek Church on Benendendorpsweg. The chuch spire, severely weakened by the shell fire and mortar hits, finally collapsed on the last day of battle.*

Above: *Memorial at Oosterbeek church to the Allied combatants.*

Left: *The Oosterbeek Perimeter. By the 20th, the British were constricted in a defensive perimeter. The remnants of the units that had been fighting in Arnhem came to the perimeter by the southern Lion, a route screened by two 6pdr anti-tank guns which knocked out a number of AFVs in an action that won Lance-Sgt John Baskeyfield of the South Staffs a posthumous VC. The battle raged around this perimeter for six days against a number of German Kampfgruppen, reinforced from the 24th by a company of 14 Tiger IIs of sPzAbt 506 (another company went to Elst), one of which was knocked out on the 25th by a combination of artillery fired from Nijmegen and anti-tank fire from the perimeter.*

A *A casualty is brought to the aid post in the Hartenstein cellar—the HQ of the British forces.*

B *The Airborne Museum Hartenstein is dedicated to the battle of Arnhem.*

C *Arnhem Aircrew Memorial (at **2** in **H**). to the memory of the Royal Air Force, Commonwealth, and United States aircrew who died during the operation. It was dedicated in 2006.*

D *Maj-Gen. Roy Urquhart commanded the British 1st AB Div during the operation.*

E *Soldiers use parachutes to signal to supply aircraft from the grounds of the Hartenstein.*

F *Memorial (at **3** in **H**):*
"To the people of Gelderland 50 years ago British & Polish Airborne soldiers fought here against overwhelming odds to open the way into Germany and bring the war to an early end. Instead we brought death and destruction for which you have never blamed us. This stone marks our admiration for your great courage, remembering especially the women who tended our wounded. In the long winter that followed your families risked death by hiding Allied soldiers and airmen, while members of the Resistance helped many to safety.
You took us then into your homes as fugitives and friends, we took you forever into our hearts. This strong bond will continue long after we are all gone."

G *Firing back at German snipers from the front balcony of the Hartenstein. He is using an American M1 carbine—a weapon he may have acquired from one of the 12 American soldiers that were present at Divisional HQ during the battle.*

H *Aerial view of Hartenstein showing (**1**) one of two 17pdr ATk guns preserved. (**4**) Sherman V Argyle of 4th Tp, A Sqn, 2nd Tank Regt, Canadian 5th Armd Div. This saw action in April 1945 when it assisted in clearing German troops to the west of Arnhem.*

To the memory of the
Royal Air Force, Commonwealth
and United States Aircrew
who died on
Operation Market Garden,
September 1944.

John 15:13
Greater love hath
no man than this, that
a man lay down his life
for his friends.

"In memoria aeterna"

TO THE PEOPLE OF GELDERLAND

50 years ago British & Polish Airborne soldiers fought here
against overwhelming odds to open the way into Germany
and bring the war to an early end. Instead we brought death
and destruction for which you have never blamed us.
This stone marks our admiration for your great courage
remembering especially the women who tended our wounded.
In the long winter that followed your families risked death
by hiding Allied soldiers and airmen while members of the
Resistance helped many to safety.

You took us then into your homes as fugitives and friends,
we took you forever into our hearts.
This strong bond will continue
long after we are all gone.

1944 ~ SEPTEMBER ~ 1994

There had been a chance, when the Polish Brigade dropped successfully, that a speedy crossing of the river could have held the perimeter until 43rd Wessex Division could cross. Three elements militated against this. First, the absence of the ferry, cut loose by the ferryman so that it couldn't be used by the Germans: without it, and in absence of other suitable boats, it was difficult to organize a crossing. Second, the loss of the high ground (the Westerbouwing) on the north bank on the 21st made a crossing even more tenuous. An attack by Pz Kompanie 224 (a flamethrower unit) took the heights, although they lost three tanks to PIATs fired by Pte George Everington. Third, there were continued holdups in getting XXX Corps through, thanks to the German blocking force with heavy armor (including King Tigers). The opportunity slipped away as 43rd Division first struggled to move up along Hell's Highway, then struggled to get from Nijmegen to Driel.

In Oosterbeek, the defenders were running short of supplies. Heavy flak and Luftwaffe fighters meant that few supplies got through. The resupply drop on September 21 lost 19 aircraft and delivered only 11 tons out of 273 dropped; that on the 22nd was canceled due to the weather. On the 23rd 11 aircraft were shot down and less than ten percent of the supplies recovered; on the 24th and 25th nothing was recovered.

Urquhart sent his GSO1 and chief engineer over the river to talk to the Poles and 43rd Div on the 22nd. They returned on the 23rd with the info that the Poles and 130 Bde would cross on the 24th. However, it was not to be. After two days of constant attacks through heavy shelling and mortaring, on the 25th the decision to pull out came across the water. Operation Berlin saw the division withdraw across the river on the night of 25/26th. It was accomplished in rain and wind: for once the weather worked for the Allies. Some 2,400 got across leaving behind them some 8,000 of their comrades—1,485 dead and 6,525 prisoners.

A *Probably taken on the 21st, this mortar team is from 23 Mortar Pl, Support Coy, 1st Border Regt.*

B *Maj. "Jock" Neill, commanding C Coy, 1st Bn Border Regt, and (right) Lt. John McCartney commanding No 28 MMG Pl in a slit trench awaiting the next German attack. Neill, already wounded, would win the DSO for his courage and leadership.*

C *After crossing back over the Rhine, the survivors stacked their weapons, had a meal, and the slept! This group sorting through weapons is at the Pagoda Missionary College in Driel.*

D *Two glider pilots looking for snipers in a school on Kneppehoutweg, in the southern section of the perimeter. Note the supply container in the doorway.*

E *Resupply drop on September 21 (for photo of canister see p23). 64 Stirlings and 53 Dakotas flew in five missions but were depleted badly by the Luftwaffe, losing 19 Daks and 16 Stirlings*

F *75mm howitzer of 2nd Bty, D Tp, Light Regiment fires east in support of the Lonsdale Force.*

Chapter 5
BATTLE OF THE BULGE

Previous Page: *L–R, Sgt. Lyle Greene, S/Sgt. Joseph De Mott, and Pfc. Fred Mozzoni heading toward the front north of Malmedy, December 29.*

Below: *The main German attacks in the Ardennes. While much attention is paid to Peiper's* Leibstandarte *in the north, and the siege of Bastogne in the south, the deepest thrust was in the center, where* Fifth Panzerarmee *almost reached the Meuse.*

Opposite: *The photos on this page show the Arctic conditions under which much of the fighting took place, including (main photo) 44th Armd Inf Regt of 6th Armd Div, ready for an attack on the forces encircling Bastogne, and grounded artillery liaison aircraft of the 422nd FA Bn, 3rd Armd Div.*

Hitler's last gamble saw him squander many of his best remaining divisions and equipment in a counterattack on the Western Front that was doomed to failure. This assessment, some 70 years after the event, may be accurate, but it belittles one of the greatest feats of American arms in the European Theater. Undoubtedly, once the Allies were able to organize themselves after the shock of the initial attack, bring their air superiority into play, and starve the attackers of fuel and materiel, the German forces ground to a halt. As they were pushed back to Germany in January 1945, they left behind tanks, halftracks, munitions, and men they could ill afford to lose in their later homeland defense. But they had been within sight of the Meuse; they had caused one of the largest surrenders of US forces since the civil war; and they had caused some 108,347 American casualties, including 19,246 killed, 62,489 wounded and 26,612 captured and missing, the most in any ETO engagement.

Four German armies were involved: two to hold the flanks—the Fifteenth under Gen. Gustav-Adolf von Zangen in the north and the Seventh, of four infantry divisions, under Gen. Erich Brandenberger in the south—and the two main attacking forces: the Sixth Panzerarmee, made up of the 1st SS-Pz Div *Leibstandarte* and 12th SS-Pz Div *Hitlerjugend*, under SS Gen. Sepp Dietrich, in the north and the Fifth Panzerarmee under Gen. Hasso von Manteuffel in the center.

They were beaten in the end by the huge men and materiel superiority of the Allies, but the seeds of defeat were sown on the northern flank, the Elsenborn Ridge, where the 99th Inf Div and 291st ECB held the Sixth Panzerarmee and gave other units—in particular 7th Armored and 82nd Airborne—sufficient time to move into defensive positions around St. Vith.

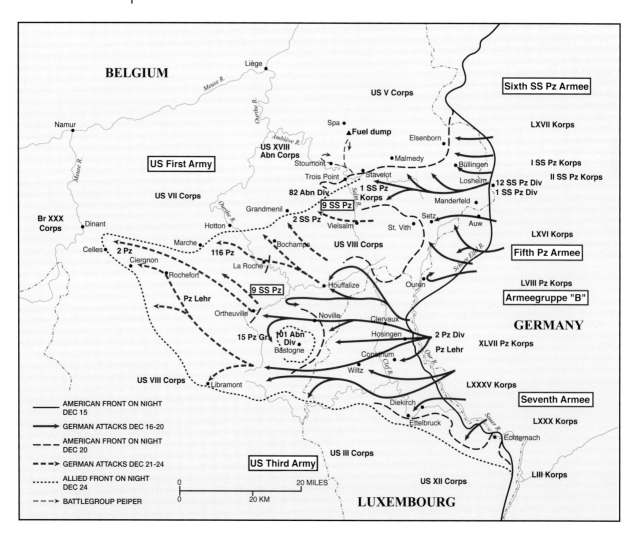

DECEMBER 16, 1944
1200Z

The German offensive took place during the worst winter in Europe for 50 years.

"Weather is a weapon the German army used with success, especially in the Ardennes offensive" said von Rundstedt, the German commander-in-chief in the west, following his capture five months later. On December 16, as the weather map (**Inset left**) shows, the fronts and pressure centers at the start of the battle led to a southerly flow over the Ardennes and the airmass was modified cold polar maritime. With the prolonged airflow from the Atlantic, plenty of moisture was available to support the fog and stratus that continued for several days. As the front that was over England on the 16th approached Belgium, rain began. Heavy mists hung over the forest. However, the weather broke for five days beginning on December 23 as a high pressure area extended east–west across Northern Europe from England to Russia. Cold polar continental air was flowing into the Ardennes and Eifel with the easterly winds that prevailed on the southern edge of the high. This high was composed of the merging of the strong Russian high and a polar maritime high that moved in from the Atlantic on December 18. By the 23rd the polar continental air had completely modified the air over the combat zone. Decreasing cloudiness allowed Allied air power to break the back of the German offensive. Once more the bombers and fighter-bombers could fly. The Bastogne air drop began with the first of the carriers dropping its six para-packs at 11:50.

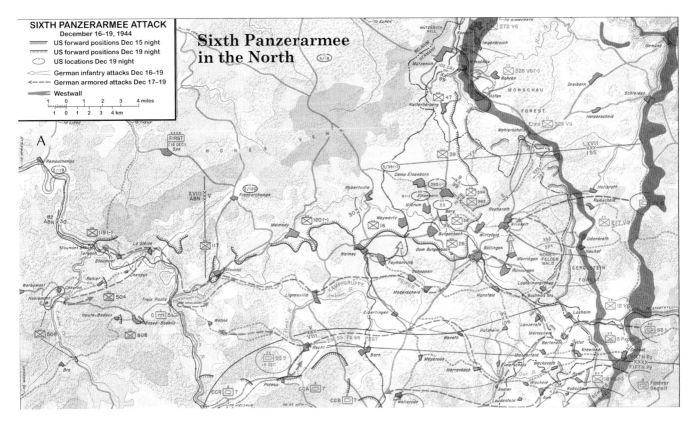

SIXTH PANZERARMEE ATTACK
December 16–19, 1944

US forward positions Dec 15 night
US forward positions Dec 19 night
US locations Dec 19 night
German infantry attacks Dec 16–19
German armored attacks Dec 17–19
Westwall

Sixth Panzerarmee
in the North

A *The northern arm of the offensive struck the Elsenborn Ridge, where three US infantry divisions—the 1st, 2nd, and 99th—bore the brunt of the fighting.*

B *A Panther of 12th Pz Regt burns outside Krinkelt on December 18.*

C *Two knocked-out Panthers of I.SS-Panzer Regiment 12 in Krinkelt. On December 18 elements of 99th Inf Div, reinforced by 2nd Inf, attacked in fog. The Panthers were easy meat for the bazooka teams.*

D, E, F *Memorials to the three main units involved in the defense: the "Battle Babes" of 99th Div (**D**) near Krinkelt Church, the 2nd Div in Krinkelt (**E**), and 1st Division (**F**) on the roundabout on the road from Büllingen to Bütgenbach.*

G *US artillery provided essential support to break up German attacks, particularly around the critical twin villages of Krinkelt and Rocherath. Here shellcases from the 105mm guns of the 38th FA Bn, assigned to 2nd Inf Div, litter the snowy landscape.*

H *M7 105mm HMC seen on December 20 at a road junction leading to the Elsenborn Ridge.*

Opposite, Above: *C Coy, 16th Inf Regt, 1st Inf Div. The Big Red One had been sent to a rest camp on December 12, but was sent to Camp Elsenborn when the German offensive began. The 16th took up positions near Robertville and Waywertz. From there the regiment spent nearly a month engaged in firefights with 1st SS-Pz and 3rd Fallshirmjäger Divs before moving onto the offensive.*

Opposite, Inset: *Ninth Air Force officers pose by a Panther knocked out in front of the Hotel des Ardennes in Ligneuville on December 17. It had been commanded by SS-Untersturmführer Arndt Fisher.*

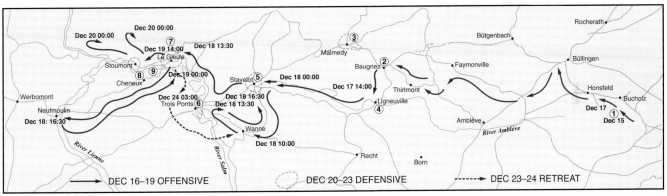

Opposite, Below: *A classic Ardennes photo, showing one of sPzAbt 501's King Tigers on its way to Lanzerath, passing a column of captured soldiers from the US 99th Inf Div.*

Top Left: *Elements of US 30th Inf Div guard a demolition-prepared bridge in Malmedy, December 22. The city was bombed repeatedly by the USAAF over the next three nights, killing some 200 civilians.*

Above: *Kampfgruppe Peiper struggled to find a path through the narrow lanes and found many of the key bridges blown. Photos of locations 1, 3, 4, and 9 are on this spread; 2, Baugnez, pp120–121; 5 Stavelot, pp122–123; 6, 7 and 8, Trois Ponts, the Château de Froidcourt, and Cheneux pp124–125; and 9 La Gleize pp126–127.*

Left: *Bazooka men of 82nd Airborne's C Coy, 325th GIR, await Kampfgruppe Peiper on December 20 at Werbomont.*

119

Opposite: *The American War Memorial at Baugnez crossroads. The tablet reads:*

"To the memory of the United States soldiers who while prisoners of war were massacred by Nazi troops on this spot on 17 December 1944."

The black markers identify the 80 dead.

Opposite, Inset: *Memorial at Ligneuville where, later the same day, eight soldiers from 9th Armd Div were murdered.*

Above: *What actually happened at Malmedy has been debated since 1944. It seems unlikely that Peiper himself gave direct orders to initiate the massacre, but postwar attempts to obfuscate the issue cannot hide the enormity of what happened. The effects were felt throughout the US Army and retribution was taken. Sgt. Howard J. Brodie was a staff artist at* Yank *magazine and drew this emotive sketch after talking to survivors.*

Left: *After the massacre at Malmedy, 84 bodies were found. They had been cold-bloodedly murdered by the SS.*

Above and Above Right: *Stavelot's bridge across the Amblève was the scene of heavy fighting on December 18 and later. Having advanced from Ligneuville on the 17th, at first light on the 18th Peiper attacked down the hill into Stavelot (1) along the Chemin de Château. He took the bridge (3), crossed the river, and headed towards Trois Ponts (7). Later that day 1st Bn, 117th Inf Regt, 30th Inf Div, who had fought against Leibstandarte in Normandy—retook the bridge, cutting Peiper off. Attempts to retake the bridge came to naught, and it was blown later by the defenders. There are a number of differences between the then and now scenes: at 2 in the then image can be seen the knocked out Tiger II (turret number 222) and a Schwimmwagen; the large building at 4 is no longer there, a M3A1 White halftrack (see inset) serves as a memorial to the fighting in the area that continued into January. However, the nearby building at (5) remains.*

Left: *In Stavelot's Rue Haut Rivage (6) Kampfgruppe Peiper lost King Tiger turret number 105, the mount of company commander SS-Obersturmführer Jürgen Wessel of sPzAbt 501. It was hit on the mantlet, reversed into a building and was immobilized.*

Right: *The bridge at Stavelot as depicted by US Army war artist Bernard Arnest.*

Top: *Cheneux as depicted by war artist Harrison Standley.*

Above and Below: *The road from La Gleize to Stoumont. At* **1** *the Château de Froidcourt (see photo above).*

Opposite: *The Kampfgruppe reached Trois Ponts on the road from Stavelot (***2***) looking for a bridge across the Amblève, but the 51st ECB blew both it (***5***) and the two bridges over the Salm (***6 and 7***). A*

plaque—**4** positioned at **3**—commends C Coy, 51st ECB for their bravery. The first bridge (**6**) was close; the other (**7** on map) was some way south and Peiper had sent a small force of PzKpfw IVs (6 and 7 Coys, 1st SS-Pz Regt and 3rd Coy 1st SS-Pz Pionier Abt) past Wanne to come round on it from behind. They arrived too late. With his way barred, Peiper was forced to head north and, reaching La Gleize, tried to route via Cheneux and over the Lienne Creek. Held

up by an air attack, the Kampfgruppe arrived at the bridge to see it blown up by 291st ECB. Peiper backtracked to La Gleize where he received good news— there was a small reinforcing column with some fuel tankers—and the bad news that Stavelot had fallen to the Americans. The only way was forward towards Stoumont and a route to the Meuse via Huy. The attack would commence on December 19.

1

2

4

Dedicated To

Company C
51st Engineer Combat Battalion
17-21 December, 1944

The engineers at the Battle of Trois Ponts
stopped elements of the Sixth German
Panzer Army from breaking out to the
Meuse River, until reinforced by the
82nd Airborne Division.

3

5

6

Peiper turns north to La Gleize
to Stavelot
Peiper advance

River Amblève

⑤
Amblève bridge
Petit Spai bridge
E Co. 505th PIR

Salm bridge
Anti-tank gun

Wanne Heights

⑥
River Salm ⑦

Lower Salm bridge

TROIS PONTS
December, 1944

G Co 505th PIR

ICI

At 07:00 on December 19, Peiper advanced towards Stoumont. Initially, the attack went well albeit against stern defense by the 3rd Bn, 119th Inf Regt, 30th Inf Div who had been reinforced by 10 M4s earlier that morning. By 11:00 the 119th had been forced back to Stoumont Station where the 1st Bn, 119th Inf Regt, reinforced by the 740th Tank Bn (the 119th's Combat Journal identifies a company of mediums and SP TDs) attacked and pushed Peiper back. The battle raged in Stoumont for the next two days, particularly around the key location, the Stoumont St. Edouard Sanatorium, until, on the afternoon of the 21st, Peiper pulled his force back and set up a defensive position around La Gleize. They fought until all fuel and food had gone, the only attempt to airdrop supplies falling mainly into American hands. Early in the morning of the 24th Peiper and some thousand men left a rearguard and the wounded and made a break for German lines, which they achieved successfully on the 25th. The vehicles left behind are analysed carefully in Duel in the Mist 3 and included King Tigers 104 and 204 (**Opposite, Inset Left**), and in the near vicinity were four more King Tigers—213, 218, 221, and 334. In total Peiper left behind over 50 tanks and SP guns and 70 halftracks.

Today, the museum at La Gleize boasts a number of recovered exhibits including one of these King Tigers (turret number 213, top), which ended up outside the museum (**1**), originally the presbytery that was used as an aid station. The town hall (**2**) had been used as a command post. The US Army had intended to take King Tiger 213 home in July 1945, but the story goes that it was saved by the intervention of a local woman and a bottle of cognac. 213 was instead towed to the village square, and in August 1951, the Belgian Army moved it to its present position near the churchyard. The damage on the glacis was caused after capture when infantrymen tried to penetrate it.

Opposite, Inset Right: One of the 26 monuments in the Ardennes that show the limit of the German advance.

127

We left Dr. Van Heely and the 113rd FA Bn at Maastricht. He and the 30th Division were involved in the battle for Aachen and on the River Roer after which the division rested. The reports from the Ardennes immediately saw them ordered south toward Eupen to prepare for a counterattack to the southeast However, the advance of Kampfgruppe Peiper changed everything. At 16:30 on December 17 the division moved off by combat teams; en route, the leading combat team—the 117th Infantry—was ordered to Malmedy.The next morning, further orders: one battalion was to go to Stavelot to stop the Germans from advancing north of the Amblève River.

CO of the 117th was Walter K. Johnson, who had been promoted colonel in October. He hurried his 1st Bn toward Stavelot, deploying his 2nd Bn on the ridge between Stavelot and Malmedy, and put the 3rd Battalion into Malmedy. It was too late. On the morning of December 18 the Germans attacked and took Stavelot ... and reports came in of German armor moving north from Trois Ponts in the direction of La Gleize and Stoumont.

At this critical juncture, the 30th Division did what it had done at Mortain: it took the fight to the enemy, retaking Stavelot (thanks to the timely arrival of air support) and destroying the bridge thereby cutting Peiper's lines of communications and logistics. His force would come up against the rest of 30th Division at Stoumont and be held up long enough for 82nd Airborne to join the battle. Heavy fighting saw the Kampfgruppe knocked back and, out of fuel, Peiper and his men abandoned their vehicles and melted away heading back to their lines.

Top Left: Heely's photo of the Baugnez crossroads (see also pp120–121) where the Malmedy massacre took place.

Center Left: A howitzer of B Battery, 113th FA Bn, in a camouflaged position at Ster, just north of Stavelot.

Left: No 2 gun of A Battery in full recoil—another view from Ster.

Right: *A steel-wheeled Panther, one of a number abandoned or knocked out during the fighting around La Gleize.*

Center Right: *This Tiger II, turret number 204 (see also previous page), ran out of fuel and was abandoned and captured at La Gleize. It was refueled by US troops who drove it a few hundred yards to the south and abandoned it after it stalled.*

Below Right: *M114 155mm howitzer of A Battery, 113th FA Bn having moved to Recht, northeast of St. Vith, January 1945. The M114 first saw action in North Africa in 1942. It used two-part ammunition (a projectile and a separate bagged propellant charge). While it mostly fired HE, it could also fire illumination, smoke or white phosphorus shells. Over 4,000 of the M1 and M1A1 were produced—the M1A1 was issued in 1944 and differed from the M1 in being made from strengthened steel and with air rather than electrical brakes. The howitzer had a range of 16,000 yards firing HE; the smoke would go out to 9,700 yards, and the illumination to 7,000. A good crew (usually 11 men) could fire 40 rounds a minute—with great accuracy. It served with the US Army into the Vietnam War.*

Fifth Panzerarmee in the Center

In his definitive official history of the Battle of the Bulge, Hugh M. Cole talks about "Cannae in the Schnee Eifel" referring back to Hannibal's brilliant double-encirclement of the Roman Army on August 2, 216 BC. General der Panzertruppen Hasso von Manteuffel's Fifth Panzerarmee encircled the US forces on the Schnee Eifel—primarily the 106th Inf Div—and forced the surrender of two regiments on December 19: America's only significant defeat in the ETO saw upward of 7,000 enter captivity. St. Vith was the next objective and the battle for the town was intense. To the north of St. Vith, the left flank of *Leibstandarte* took Poteau and then struck north, attempting to fight its way to the beleaguered Kampfgruppe Peiper. Further south, Manteuffel's LVIII Pz and XLVII Korps were breaking through the 28th Inf Div toward Bastogne. St. Vith finally fell on the 21st, the defenders escaping west through a corridor held open by 82nd Airborne. The Germans may have won a significant tactical victory, but the defenders of St. Vith, particularly the 7th Armored and remnants of the 106th, had derailed their schedule, so much so that von Manteuffel told Hitler that they should return to the Westwall. Nevertheless, the German advance continued but it had to fight for every inch of ground, and every crossroads saw a pitched battle until Fifth Panzerarmee was halted close to the Meuse, where British troops were involved at the close.

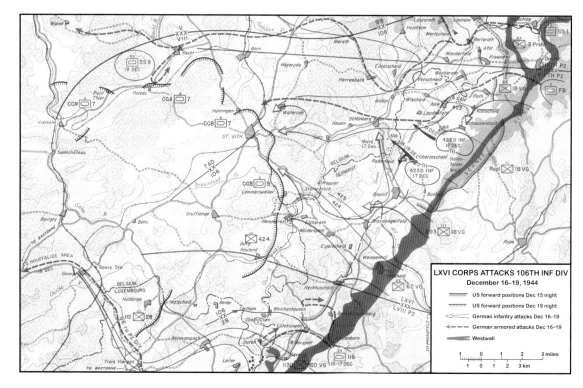

Opposite and Left: *All quiet in St. Vith in September, two months before the offensive, as a 7th Armored halftrack negotiates the winding streets. After it was captured by the Germans, the town was bombed heavily on December 25 and 26 (left) by the USAAF and by RAF Bomber Command.*

Center Left and Right: *Memorials to the 106th Division (Right) and the 168th ECB. The 106th were encircled on the Schnee Eifel losing two of their regiments to captivity; the remnants joined the defenders of St. Vith. The 168th ECB fought as part of Combat Command B 7th Armd Div.*

Below: *Vehicles of 48th Inf Bn, 7th Armd Div in St. Vith. The division was fundamental to the defense of St. Vith and helped delay the German advance before withdrawing west of the Salm River on December 23. The 7th then took part in the battles around Manhay. CCB 7th Armd Div*

"By their epic stand, without prepared defenses and despite heavy casualties ... inflicted crippling losses and imposed great delay upon the enemy by a masterful and grimly determined defense"

won a Presidential Unit Citation. After defending Manhay and Grandmenil the division was taken out of the line to refit before spearheading the retaking of St. Vith, January 20–28, 1945.

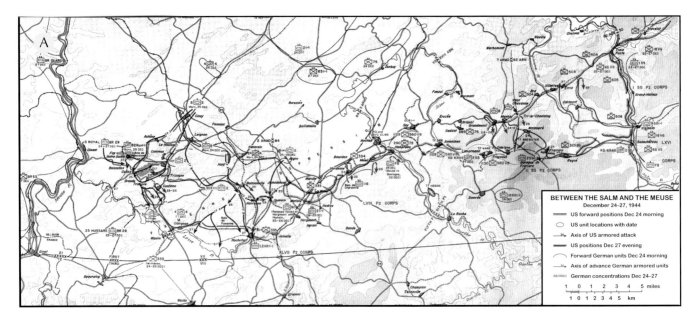

BETWEEN THE SALM AND THE MEUSE
December 24–27, 1944

US forward positions Dec 24 morning
US unit locations with date
Axis of US armored attack
US positions Dec 27 evening
Forward German units Dec 24 morning
Axis of advance German armored units
German concentrations Dec 24–27

1 0 1 2 3 4 5 miles
1 0 1 2 3 4 5 km

LE CHAR INVINCIBLE
LE COURAGE INVINCIBLE

THE AMERICAN 7th ARMORED DIVISION
AND ATTACHED UNITS
HEADQUARTERED IN VIELSALM
DURING THE CRUCIAL PERIOD
OF THE GERMAN OFFENSIVE OF THE ARDENNES
IN 1944 HELD THE IMPORTANT CENTER OF ST. VITH
PREVENTING ANY ADVANCE AND ANY EXPLOITATION
ON THIS MAIN LINE
THUS FRUSTRATING THE GERMAN OFFENSIVE
BY ITS SACRIFICE PERMITTING
THE LAUNCHING OF THE ALLIED COUNTER-OFFENSIVE

ST. VITH, BELGIUM   DEDICATED
17-23 DEC. 1944   9 JUNE 1984

PRESENTED
BY THE SEVENTH ARMORED DIVISION ASSOCIATION
IN HONOR OF ALL WHO FOUGHT SO VALIANTLY AT
ST. VITH

A *The fall of St. Vith saw some 15,000 men and about a hundred tanks escape to bolster 82nd Airborne in the defense. Sixth Panzerarmee chased them, attacking in a front from Vielsalm and the Salm River to the crossroads at Baraque. By the night of December 23, 2nd SS Panzer had taken the Baraque de Fraiture crossroads, and their next objective was the Manhay crossroads five miles away.*

B *US 7th Armd Div defensive position, Vielsalm, December 23.*

C *A memorial to 7th Armd Div in Vielsalm. Zirguezi.*

D *2nd Bn, 325th GIR, 82nd Airborne on December 20. Originally planned to defend Bastogne, when 101st Airborne were assigned there, 82nd was sent north to Werbomont. The 325th defended the crossroads at Baraque dc Fraiture. A good story on www. ww2-airborne.us tells of a sergeant in a tank destroyer who spotted a GI of F Coy, 325th GIR. The GI looked up and asked,*
"Are you looking for a safe place?"
"Yeah," answered the tanker.
"Well buddy," he drawled, "just pull your tank in behind me... I'm the 82nd Airborne and this is as far as the bastards are going!"

E *Memorial dedicated to the men of the 325th GIR, 82nd Airborne.*

F *Early January 1945 and a 2nd Armd column led by an M36 tank destroyer makes its way northwards back toward Dochamps.*

G *GIs dig foxholes on the front line just past Amonines, January 4, 1945.*

H *In memory of John T. Graham, Everett W. Christensen, Isaac Duhon, and John McMahon, gallant soldiers of the 82nd Recon Bn, 2nd Armd Div, killed in combat in January 1945 for the liberation of Samrée.*

The area around Manhay, Erezée, and Grandmenil saw intense fighting around Christmas 1944. 7th Armd had taken up positions around Manhay on the 24th. The 2nd SS-Pz Div (Das Reich) attacked at 21:00 on Christmas Eve. The defenders were deceived by a Judas Goat Sherman leading the enemy column and Manhay was taken. Gen. Hodges insisted that it should be retaken, so 2nd Bn, 424th Inf Regt and CCA, 7th Armd, attacked but were badly mauled. The fighting spread to Grandmenil but in the end, 3rd Bn, 517th PIR took the village in the early hours of the 27th.

A, B, and C *Das Reich* lost a number of Panthers in the heavy fighting around Manhay. Seven were left around the Bomal–Manhay–Grandmenil area, some destroyed, others out of fuel and others bogged in marshy ground. One was lost at the cross-roads, and later bulldozed off the road; another threw a track; a third was abandoned in a ditch to the north of the main road. Four, including turret number 407, were lost in the field to the south of the road. 407, its suspension damaged and missing its muzzle-brake, today is a memorial at Grandmenil crossroads (**B**).

D A well-camouflaged 3rd Armd M4 near Manhay.

E Memorial stone dedicated to the 238th ECB along the Grandmenil–Manhay road.

Left: *Shermans of 3rd Armd waiting for a track to be cleared near Manhay and Houffalize.*

Below: *A Das Reich Panther knocked out by the 289th Regt, 75th Inf Div, near Grandmenil. Arriving in Britain on November 22, the division was rushed to the Ourthe River on December 23 before advancing to Grandmenil on January 5. They relieved 82nd Airborne along the Salm River on January 8, and moved into the attack on January 17 when they took Vielsalm.*

B

C

Right and Below: *West of Manhay, the story was the same at Soy, Ménil, Humain, and Rochefort. Initial German gains were blocked by resolute defense. These Panthers were knocked out at Humain during a three-day battle between US 2nd Armd and 4th Cavalry Group and, on the German side, Panzer Lehr, which was replaced by 9th Pz Div transferred from the Netherlands. 2nd Armd's accurate artillery fire, Allied air support, and finally flame-throwing Crocodile tanks of the Scottish Fife and Forfar Yeomanry ended the battle.*

Above and Above Right: *The infiltration of Allied lines by special forces wearing American military uniforms was not as widespread as the fear and rumor that abounded. Cole mentions a jeep of such saboteurs captured by a British post at Dinant. Here (**Top**), a dead German in American uniform and (**Top Right**) military police attached to the 84th Inf Div halt and interrogate traffic at a vital crossroads directly north of Marche at Baillonville.*

Right: *The closest the German attack came to the Meuse was around December 24, when elements of 2nd Pz Div were about five miles from the Meuse at Foy Notre-Dame and Celles close to Dinant, where refugees flooded across the river. But the wheels were beginning to come off the offensive. Bastogne had not fallen and Patton's Third Army was rolling northward. Montgomery had assumed command of the northern forces and as von Manteuffel said postwar,*

> *"turned a series of isolated actions into a coherent battle fought according to a clear and definite plan. It was his refusal to engage in premature and piecemeal counterattacks which enabled the Americans to gather their reserves and frustrate the German attempts to extend their breakthrough."*

*The 2nd Pz Div, which had been slowed around Bastogne, ran out of fuel at Celles and was destroyed by US 2nd Armd and British 29th Armd Bde (**Below**).*

Below Right: *A British Sherman Firefly patrols the Meuse at Namur.*

Left: *Infantrymen of Easy Coy, 2nd Bn, 41st Regt, 2nd Armd advance in the attack on Humain.*

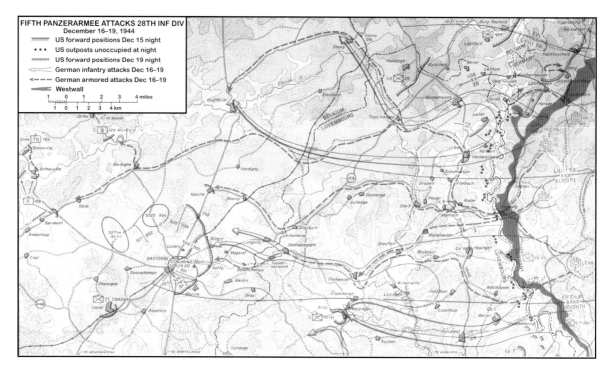

FIFTH PANZERARMEE ATTACKS 28TH INF DIV
December 16–19, 1944

〰〰〰 US forward positions Dec 15 night
• • • US outposts unoccupied at night
· · · · · US forward positions Dec 19 night
◁───── German infantry attacks Dec 16–19
◁─ ─ ─ German armored attacks Dec 16–19
▰▰▰▰ Westwall

The southern sector of the Fifth Panzerarmee's front saw 28th Inf Div attacked by LVIII and XLVII Pz Korps, which included armored thrusts by the 116th and 2nd Pz Divs, on December 16. Dogged defense slowed up the German advance but by the time the 28th was withdrawn for reorganization on December 22, it had won time to allow Bastogne to be reinforced by Brig-Gen. McAuliffe and the 101st Airborne along with elements of the 10th Armored. On December 22, the general made his famous reply to German suggestions that Bastogne surrender: "Nuts!" On the 23rd, the weather was good enough to allow air resupply of food, medicine, and weaponry and on the 26th, Patton's Third Army broke the deadlock as 4th Armored arrived. North of Bastogne, the 116th Pz Div had reached Houffalize on December 19 before striking north to take Samrée, Dochamps, and Verdenne by Christmas Eve. Heavy fighting halted the German attacks and allowed the Allies to build up sufficient strength to counterattack—US First Army on the east bank of the Ourthe and BR 6th Airborne and 53rd Divisions on the west. There was still two weeks of hard fighting in awful wintry conditions before Third and First armies linked up at Houffalize on January 16, and another week before the "Bulge" was finally reduced to its pre-December 16 position.

This Page: *Houffalize was taken by 116th Panzer Division on December 19 but this Panther G, original turret number 111 now marked 401, probably from I./16.Pz Regt, was knocked out later as the First and Third Armies fought to reduce the "Bulge." Local accounts suggest it was toppled into the river as a result of bombing and that the crew died as a result. The Panther was recovered from the Ourthe by engineers on September 20, 1948, and has been moved up the hill to become a memorial, as the modern photos show.*

139

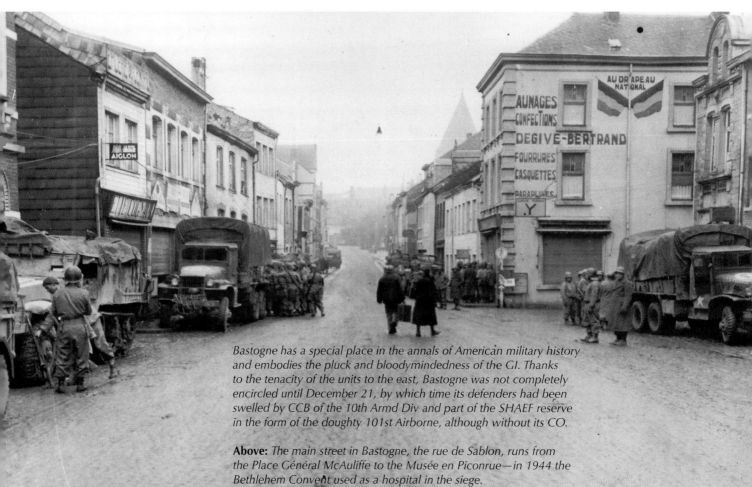

Bastogne has a special place in the annals of American military history and embodies the pluck and bloodymindedness of the GI. Thanks to the tenacity of the units to the east, Bastogne was not completely encircled until December 21, by which time its defenders had been swelled by CCB of the 10th Armd Div and part of the SHAEF reserve in the form of the doughty 101st Airborne, although without its CO.

Above: The main street in Bastogne, the rue de Sablon, runs from the Place Général McAuliffe to the Musée en Piconrue—in 1944 the Bethlehem Convent used as a hospital in the siege.

Above and Below: *Then and now aerial views of Bastogne.*
*1 identifies the road running north and is visible at the lower
left of the aerial recon photo. 2 identifies the main square (see
pp142–143), and 3 the course of the rue de Sablon.*

Above and Top: *Refugees evacuating Bastogne. They are in the main square now named after Brig-Gen. Anthony McAuliffe.*

Right and Opposite, Top
The same scene today, the view blocked by Bastogne's Tourist Information Center also prominent in the aerial view of the square (1).

Opposite, Below: *Memorials in the square are to 11th Armd (2) and Gen. McAuliffe (3).*

GENERAL
McAULIFFE

A and B *Bois Jacques—Jack's Wood—Band of Brothers. The plaque on the monument (right) reads:*

"May the world never forget. In the wood behind this monument, on 18 December 1944 'E' Company of the 506th PIR 101st Airborne Division dug their foxholes in the Bois Jacques Woods as part of the defense perimeter of Bastogne City that was soon to be surrounded by several enemy divisions. The circumstances were dreadful with constant mortar, rocket and artillery fire, snow fall, temperatures below -28 Celsius at night with little food and ammunition. The field hospital had been captured so little medical help was available. On December 24th the 'E' Company position was attacked at dawn by about 45 enemy soldiers. The attack failed and 'E' Company held their position with 1 casualty against 23 of the enemy. The position of 'E' Company was twice bombed and strafed by American P-47s. During the periods of January 9th and January 13th 'E' Company suffered its most casualties ending with the attack and capture of Foy on January 13th. 8 were killed in Foy and 6 earlier. During the whole period 32 were wounded and 21 were evacuated with cold weather illnesses. In many units involved in the defense of Bastogne the casualties were even greater. This monument is dedicated to all that fought and is symbolic of what happened to other units during the Battle of the Bulge. Airborne Always"

C *East of Bastogne in an area taken by 320th Regt, 35th Inf Div, this grave marks the final resting place of a German Fallschirmjäger from the 5th Division, part of German Seventh Armee. Attacked by US Third Army's 4th Armd Div, the Fallschirmjäger took part in the final attack on the town on Christmas Eve, but were pushed back to the German border.*

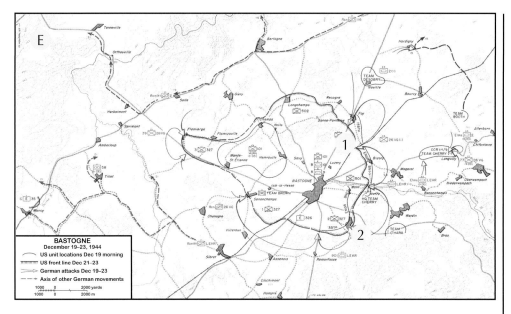

BASTOGNE
December 19–23, 1944
⌒ US unit locations Dec 19 morning
⊥⊥⊥⊥ US front line Dec 21–23
⟶ German attacks Dec 19–23
- - → Axis of other German movements
1000 0   2000 yards
1000 0   2000 m

D *There are a number of tank turrets on pedestals around Bastogne. This one—a T23 turret with a 10th Armd patch—is on the road to the Mardasson Memorial. The associated panel says:*

"The US 10th Armored Division's Combat Command B, the first major combat unit to defend Bastogne, arrived on the evening of December 18, 1944. Col William L. Roberts deployed his Combat Command in three teams: Team Desobry at Noville, Team Cherry at Neffe and Longvilly, Team O'Hara at Wardin and Marvie. After delaying the initial German advance, the remnants of these 10th Armored teams joined the 101st Airborne Division for the remainder of the siege. In recognition of their gallant actions, Combat Command B was awarded the Presidential Unit Citation."

E *The encirclement of Bastogne. (**1**) marks the location of the Easy Company memorial. Note the location of 10th Armored's teams Desobry, Cherry, and O'Hara as noted in the caption below.*

F *December 26—the day the garrison was relieved by 4th Armored—as 101st Airborne watched C-47s drop supplies. Resupply by air—particularly of ammunition—was difficult because of the weather but helped keep the garrison alive.*

G *The outskirts of Neffe (**2** on the map) by war artist Olin Dows. Dows spent a year in England before D-Day and then traveled to Normandy as part of the 166th Signal Unit. He was assigned to Bastogne in late December, and witnessed the siege of the city.*

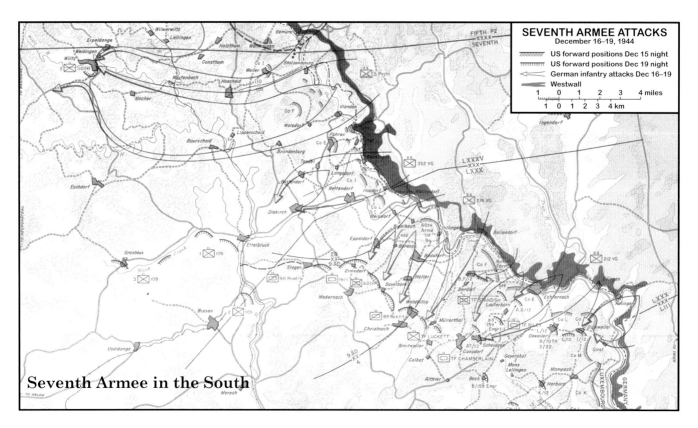

Seventh Armee in the South

SEVENTH ARMEE ATTACKS
December 16–19, 1944

▨▨▨ US forward positions Dec 15 night
▨▨▨ US forward positions Dec 19 night
◀── German infantry attacks Dec 16–19
▬▬ Westwall

1 0 1 2 3 4 miles
1 0 1 2 3 4 km

Above: *The German Seventh Army, made up of the 212th, 256th, and 352nd VGR divisions and 5th FJR Division—with no armor or heavy weapons—had limited taskings for the operation. The attack on US 4th Inf Div positions had the benefit of surprise, but tenacious defense and excellent artillery work, along with support from 10th Armored, ensured that little ground was given. Casualties were high, but Seventh Armee was able to do little to stop Third Army, as it drove to relieve Bastogne and then north to Houffalize.*

Right: *Wiltz in Luxembourg was the command post of Gen. Norman "Dutch" Cota's 28th Inf Div from December 19. As has been seen (p138) the 28th played a valiant role in holding off the German attacks towards Bastogne. Hugh Cole sums it up, "The fall of Wiltz ended the 28th Division's delaying action before Bastogne ... without the gallant bargain struck by the 110th Infantry and its Allied units—men for time—the German plans for a coup-de-main at Bastogne would have turned to accomplished fact."*

Inset: *Memorials to 10th Armored at Berdorf (**1**) and various divisions including the 4th at Osweiler (**2**).*

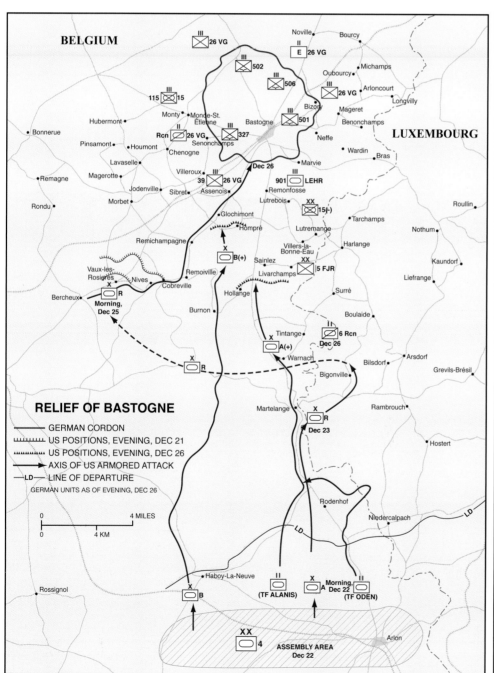

BELGIUM

LUXEMBOURG

RELIEF OF BASTOGNE

- —————— GERMAN CORDON
- ⊔⊔⊔⊔⊔⊔ US POSITIONS, EVENING, DEC 21
- ▴▴▴▴▴▴ US POSITIONS, EVENING, DEC 26
- ————▶ AXIS OF US ARMORED ATTACK
- —LD— LINE OF DEPARTURE

GERMAN UNITS AS OF EVENING, DEC 26

0   4 MILES
0   4 KM

Above Left: *1Lt. Charles Boggess, Cpl. Milton Dickerman and Pvts. James G. Murphy, Hubert S. Smith, and Harold Hafner—the happy crew of Cobra King, 37th Tank Bn, 4th Armd—pose after their M4A3E2 "Jumbo" Sherman assault tank had led the armored column into Bastogne. It would take two weeks to push the Germans east of Bastogne, and the battle officially ended more than a week later, on January 17. The 37th earned a Presidential Unit Citation for its relief of the city.*

Above: *A 4th Armd M5 light tank moves toward Bastogne, December 27.*

Left: *Elements of Third Army punched through to Bastogne from the southwest. They met the 326th Engineers at around 16:50 on December 26. A day later Gen. Maxwell D. Taylor reached Bastogne with the 4th Armored and resumed command of the 101st Airborne. The battle didn't stop there: immediately after the siege had been lifted, Third Army moved on northwards to crush the remnants of the attacking force. It would subsequently eliminate the Saar-Palatinate triangle*

Above: *84th Inf Div of First Army meets 11th Armd of Third Army in Houffalize on January 16. The Battle of the Bulge is almost over: the invasion of Germany is about to begin.*

Right: *Lt-Gen. George Patton (right), Lt-Col. Steve A.Chappuis (center, commanding 2/502nd PIR), and Brig-Gen. Anthony McAuliffe on the steps of Chateau de Rolley after Patton had given them the DSC.*

Below Right: *A 4th Armd M4A3 (76mm) covers highway H4 near Bastogne.*

Opposite, Top Left: *Map showing XXX Corps involvement in the counterattack. Most of the units in the Ardennes were American, but the British played their part, 3rd RTR engaging and halting leading elements of 2nd Pz Div as they approached the Meuse, and XXX Corps taking part in the hard fighting to dislodge German forces on the west bank of the Ourthe. The infantry divisions identified here supported by the tanks of the 23rd Hussars, the Fife and Forfar and 1st Northamptonshire Yeomanry, and 144th RAC Regt.*

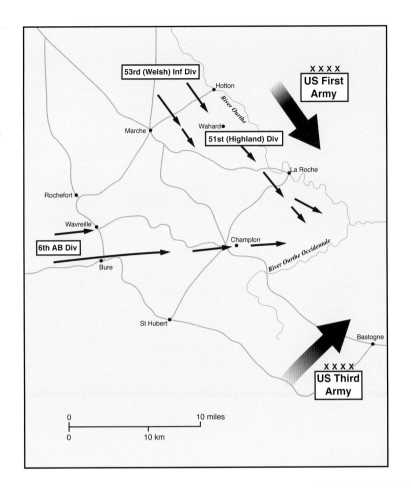

Above Right: *Fireflies of B Sqn East Riding Yeomanry, part of the 33rd Armd Bde, lining the western bank of the Ourthe river in Hotton on January 4.*

Right: *Monty inspects British 6th Airborne in the Ardennes.*

Below: *Churchills waiting to move forward to support British 53rd Division.*

YOU ARE NOW ENTERING
GERMANY
THROUGH THE COURTESY OF THE
U 6 S
6TH ARMORED DIVISION

Reaching the Rhine

Following the failure of their Ardennes Offensive, the Germans were forced to move many of their surviving forces to the east to counter a Russian offensive. The enemy left in the west, as General Patton outlined in his After Action Report, "resorted again to his policy of defending and delaying, selling space for time by shuttling troops from one threatened sector of the front to the other and reinforcing with a miscellany of units when he was able. None of these desperate moves was able to stall for long the advance of Third U.S. Army." Following the initial counterattack by First and Third Armies, Patton's men continued on, clearing the area west of the Rhine and north of the Moselle in February, taking Trier on March 2, 1945.

The next major offensive started on March 12, Operation Undertone, which saw Third and Seventh Armies combine to clear the Saar-Palatinate area and by March 24, US armies were poised to cross the Rhine. The Germans had delayed them long enough to allow sizable quantities of men and materiel to cross over into Germany before blowing the final bridge over the Rhine in this area, at Germersheim. Nevertheless, Seventh Army captured 22,000, while Patton's Third Army took more than 68,000. Combined US losses for the two armies totaled over 17,000 with over 1,500 dead, showing the grim nature of the fighting, particularly around the Westwall. It wouldn't be long until "Georgie's Boys" were over the Rhine and heading deep into Germany.

Opposite, Above Left and Right: *Third Army engineers remove explosives from the piers of the bridge over the Moselle at Trier—then and now.*

Bottom and Inset: *Infantrymen of 90th Div and tanks of 6th Armored (inset, the tankers claim resposibility!) move through the dragon's teeth, part of the Westwall defenses.*

Below: *Cover of Patton's* After Action Report *for the month of February 1945.*

Troops of 9th Durham Light Infantry enter Bakenhoven on January 16 as part of Operation Blackcock.

Chapter 6
LIBERATING
THE NETHERLANDS

Above: *A Loyd Carrier of the Prinses Irene Brigade in September 1944. Organized from those who had fled the Netherlands after its fall in 1940, the PIB landed in Normandy and initially served under the Canadian First Army. Later it joined the British Second Army, crossing into Dutch territory on September 20, 1944.*

Below Right: *Gen. H.D.G. Crerar was commander of Canadian First Army which played the major role in the liberation of the western and northern Netherlands.*

Opposite, Above: *The Germans breached many dikes to impede the Allies, as can be seen in this photograph of B-24s during Operation Market Garden.*

Opposite, Below: *British 53rd (Welsh) Division—liberated s' Hertogenbosch on October 24–27.*

The liberation of the Netherlands proved to be considerably more difficult than might have been anticipated as the Allies chased the fleeing German army across France and into Belgium. When they entered the Netherlands on September 5, the Allies were greeted as liberators—"mad Tuesday" saw the entire country rejoice, but it would be seven more hard months before the whole country was free.

First, there was the "Bridge Too Far"—the ambitious attempt to thrust into Germany through the Ruhr and the North German Plain. The German response proved that they were not ready to roll over. The attempts to broaden the Market Garden salient in Operation Aintree saw a brutal defense by young, committed Fallschirmjäger. Indeed, with the war continuing and resupply a critical problem, the Allies were forced into the difficult task of opening up Antwerp and the Scheldt. Each stage of this operation—clearing the south side of the estuary, fighting in the Breeskens pocket, on Walcheren and south Beveland—showed that they might be short of materiel and air support, but the German defenders were still determined to keep the Third Reich alive. And having won the territory they still needed to clear the Scheldt of mines.

Having cleared the Scheldt and eased their resupply problems, the Allies could have been forgiven for thinking that life was at last going to get easier. Far from it. As the weather worsened and Christmas approached, they were surprised by a huge counterattack: 200,000 men from three German armies flooded into the Ardennes. It was the Allies' turn to grit their teeth and defend each inch of ground. The German forces lost men and equipment they could not replace, but still the surrender did not come. It took Operations Blackcock, Veritable, and Grenade in early 1945 to clear the east of the country. The Canadian First Army and the Polish 1st Armored Division led the job of clearing the north and west where fighting continued until the bitter end.

The civilian casualties in this populous country were awful, and the hard winter contributed to a humanitarian nightmare exacerbated when the Germans cut off food and fuel shipments to the western provinces.

Opposite and Left: *Breda was fortunate because there were no casualties when it was liberated by Maczek's 1st Polish Armd Div on October 29, 1944, a day that is remembered each year when a large Polish contingent descends on the city. There's a monument to Maczek in the city center and the general is buried in the nearby Polish military cemetery—as with Patton, his wish was to be laid to rest with his men. The Panther (Left), beautifully restored in 2004, was presented to the city by the Poles in 1945.*

Left and Below: *It took a month to winkle out the well-protected defenders of the Scheldt Estuary and cost the Allies nearly 13,000 casualties, half of them from Canadian First Army.*

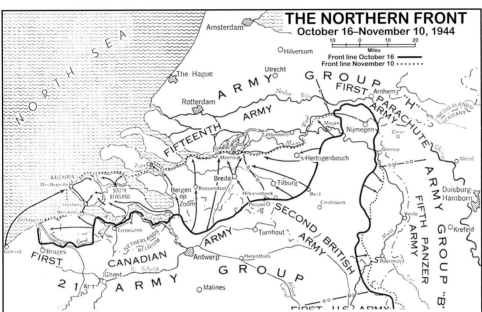

THE NORTHERN FRONT
October 16–November 10, 1944

Front line October 16 ——
Front line November 10 ·······

Above and Inset: *Today's waterfront at Westkapelle has been completely rebuilt and looks very different to its wartime equivalent.*

Right: *RAF bombers attacked the dikes of Westkapelle on the night of October 3, 1944 to flood the German occupation troops in Walcheren and make liberation easier. Unfortunately, information about the raid didn't reach the villagers and 180 were killed. The damaged dyke wasn't finally repaired until a year later—October 12, 1945.*

Opposite, Above: *The breaching of the dikes near Westkapelle meant that the Germans had to vacate the interior of the island, but stiffened the defense around the coast.*

Left: *During the attack on Westkapelle, 30 of the Close Support Squadron landing craft were lost: over 300 were killed in the action.*

Below Left: *An M4 Sherman was placed on the dyke as a memorial. The text says:*

Left panel:
 4 Commando Brigade, British Liberation Army, landed here on 1 Nov. 1944 to liberate the island.

Center panel:
 On 3rd and 29th October 1944 this dike was bombed by the Allies for the liberation of Walcheren. The city of Westkapelle was destroyed. The city of Walcheren was washed away by the sea.
 1 Nov. 1944 The landing of the Allies; 8 Nov. 1944 Walcheren was liberated; 3 Oct.1945 hole in dyke was repaired.
 WALCHEREN CAN ARISE

Right panel:
 To the greater glory of God this stone is erected by the Royal Marines in commemoration of the landing of No 4 Commando Brigade at Westkapelle on 1st November 1944.

Above and Above Right: *Little remains of prewar Westkapelle save the most obvious landmark —the lighthouse, built 1458– 1470. At 52m (171ft) tall, it is visible from 28 nautical miles away.*

Right: *LVT off Walcheren.*

Below: *Westkapelle—the Sherman shown at the bottom of p159 is at 1.*

Opposite: *The attack on Flushing (Vlissingen) was undertaken by No 4 Commando, together with 5th King's Own Scottish Borderers.*

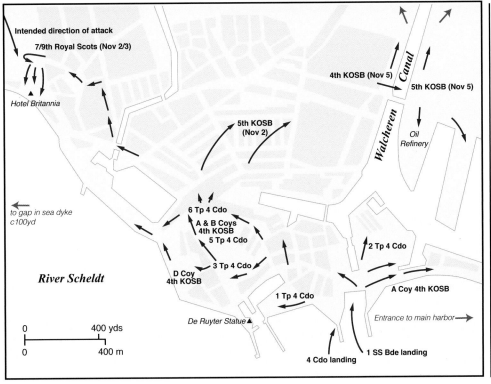

Intended direction of attack
7/9th Royal Scots (Nov 2/3)

Hotel Britannia

Canal

4th KOSB (Nov 5)

5th KOSB (Nov 5)

Walcheren

Oil Refinery

5th KOSB (Nov 2)

← *to gap in sea dyke c100yd*

6 Tp 4 Cdo

A & B Coys 4th KOSB

5 Tp 4 Cdo

2 Tp 4 Cdo

D Coy 4th KOSB

3 Tp 4 Cdo

River Scheldt

1 Tp 4 Cdo

A Coy 4th KOSB

De Ruyter Statue ▲

Entrance to main harbor →

4 Cdo landing

1 SS Bde landing

0   400 yds

0   400 m

One of the main reasons to inundate Walcheren was the sheer number of defensive structures on the island. As well as the coastal defenses, over 200 bunkers studded the interior, including a number of areas designated strongpoints. The area pictured here, between Vlissingen and Koudekerke, was set up as Stützpunkt Kolberg and its defenses included an anti-tank ditch, dragon's teeth, bomb-proof bunkers to shelter troops, store water, prepare meals and care for the injured. Ironically, in contrast to the fortifications on higher ground, Strongpoint Kolberg never had to be actively defended because it was inundated.

The bunkers visible in the main photograph and above left are of Regelbau Type 623 armed with machine-guns and with a 60° side slab—Regelbau Bunker vom Typ 623 MG Schartenstand mit Vorsatzplatte (60°).

Below left is a Type 631 bunker which was armed with a 46mm anti-tank gun. The bunkers were made mainly from concrete, that of Type 631 being 11.40m long and 14.00m wide. As well as the entrance and gas-lock there were four other rooms in the bunker: Eingangsverteidigung (entrance protection), Bereitschaftsraum für 6 Mann (ready room for six men), Munitionsraum (ammunition storage), and the Gefechtsraum (fighting room). There is an emergency exit and an open observation position in the form of a Tobruk above, as well as a location for shell cases.

Operation Aintree

Above and Center Right:
Operation Aintree was an attempt to widen the Arnhem salient towards the Maas. It included the largest tank battle in Dutch history, outside Overloon, which left the town in ruins. What was left on the battlefield formed the basis for the War Museum at Liberty Park (1) opened on May 25, 1946. Overloon Museum also includes the National War and Resistance Museum, a fantastic collection of mines and ammunition, and the remarkable, US-funded, Marshal Museum which contains over 150 historic vehicles, vessels, and aircraft. The sign at the entrance (right) reads:
"Take pause visitor, and consider that the ground you stand on was once one of the most fiercely contested sectors of the Overloon battlefield. Bitter hand-to-hand combat took place here. Many young lives, having escaped from the battlefields of Nettuno and Normandy, met their ends under these trees."

[cont on next page]

STA EEN OGENBLIK STIL BEZOEKER EN BEDENK DAT DE GROND WAAROP GIJ NU VERTOEFT EENS EEN VAN DE FELST OMSTREDEN SECTOREN WAS VAN HET SLAGVELD OVERLOON BITTER IS HIER GEVOCHTEN IN MAN TEGEN MAN GEVECHTEN VELE JONGE LEVENS AAN DE SLAGVELDEN VAN NETTUNO EN NORMANDIÉ ONTKOMEN VONDEN ONDER DEZE BOMEN HUN EINDE

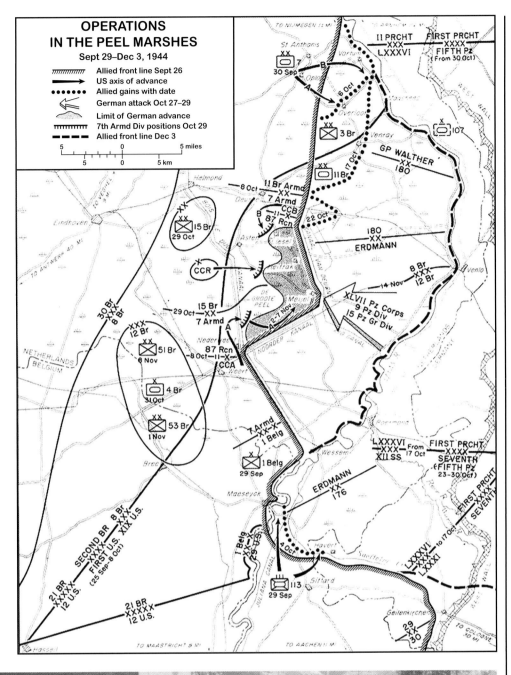

OPERATIONS IN THE PEEL MARSHES
Sept 29–Dec 3, 1944

⬚⬚⬚⬚⬚⬚⬚	Allied front line Sept 26
───▶	US axis of advance
●●●●●●	Allied gains with date
⬅═══	German attack Oct 27–29
◹◹◹◹	Limit of German advance
⬚⬚⬚⬚⬚⬚⬚	7th Armd Div positions Oct 29
━ ━ ━	Allied front line Dec 3

5   0   5 miles
5   0   5 km

*Nearby (2), stands a memorial to US 7th Armored and a restored M4A1 (**Opposite, bottom left and right**) with the markings of "Able Abe" of A Coy, 40th Tank Bn, which was disabled on October 1, 1944, during the battle. In the clearing (3) is the Commonwealth War Cemetery Overloon (see Chapter 7).*

Left: *Operation Market Garden had failed, but it left a 60-mile salient into the Netherlands. The Germans attacked the eastern side of the salient from Venlo and the Allies attacked southeast toward the Westwall. The area is known as the Peel, notable for bogs and canals, and the Germans defended determinedly blocking the Allied advance. The US 7th Armd Div opened the attack on October 30 after four days of artillery fire, but did not have sufficient force to penetrate the defenses of 107th Pz Bde and Fallschirmjäger fighting as infantry. Next to attack, on October 8, were the heavier forces of British 3rd Inf Div and 11th Armd Div. Clearing the German Maas salient would become for them "a second Caen." After desperate fighting they captured what remained of Overloon on the 14th, clearing the village with house-to-house fighting and heavy losses. Continuing southeast, the Allies advanced on Venray, fighting for every inch of ground. They continued to sustain casualties particularly at the heavily mined Loobeek creek, which was badly swollen by autumn rains. It was crossed on the 16th by 1st Bn, Royal Norfolk Regt, who raised a memorial to the fallen (see p166). Venray only fell after artillery and air bombardment: 30 of the heavy civilian casualties (some 300 all told) died on October 12 when US B-26 Marauders bombed Venray; on the 13th some 15,000 artillery shells were fired at the town in three hours. The Germans finally left the town on the 19th.*

Below Left: *British 3rd Division and supporting Sherman tanks on their way to Overloon.*

Opposite, Above and Below: *Churchill gun tanks (**Above**) and a flail (**Below**) in Overloon. The Overloon Museum has a Churchill Mk IV gun tank (Jackal of 4th Bn Coldstream Guards which was knocked out by a mine) and a flail tank with 79th Armd Div markings (**Inset Left**)—obliterated by the censor on the contemporary photo.*

Opposite, Inset Right: *The memorial to 1st Bn, Royal Norfolk Regt, is also dedicated "to all innocent victims of war, especially the 300 civilians who were killed in and around Overloon and Venray in 1944."*

Above Left: *While trying to cross the heavily mined Loobeek creek this AVRE bridgelayer was knocked out.*

Above Right: *British troops enter Venray.*

Below: *Venray today, centered around St. Petrus Banden (St. Peter in chains) church, whose tower survived a rocket attack by Typhoons before being blown up by the Germans when they left on October 19. (**Inset** 1946 view.) The excellent www.go2war2. nl/ website has detailed descriptions of the battles around Overloon and discusses why the Germans fought with such tenacity across the Netherlands. Three main points are identified: first, propaganda and education—many German soldiers still believed in ultimate victory with the new weapons playing an important role in fostering this belief. Second, honor and duty— even against the sternest odds, officers and men felt (as did their opponents) that they couldn't let their mates down. Third, and some would say the biggest difference between the two sides, the summary justice meted out to those who would not fight. One captain said in 1984,*

"... this must be crystal clear to you, I would have been put against the wall and executed. No single doubt about that. Already many men had undergone the same fate and were hung from a rope in Germany."

After Venray fell, fighting continued in the Maas salient. In late October the German XLVII Korps counterattacked around Meyel and Liessel toward Deurne, where it was stopped by a combination of US 7th Armd Div, 15th Scottish Div, and heavy artillery support. Finally, by the end of November, the German salient had withered to three small pockets: Geysteren Castle, Broekhuizen, and Blerick, a suburb of Venlo that had been turned into a fortress (see map).

Above Right: *Ram Kangaroo APCs during the assault by 15th Scottish Div on Blerick, December 3. Through lanes in minefields cleared by flails (22nd Dragoons), over an anti-tank ditch bridged by Churchill AVLBs (81st Assault Engineers), in spite of the mud, the APCs delivered their occupants (Royal Scots Fusiliers) on the outskirts of Blerick, which fell quickly thanks to an inspired attack plan by General Cummings-Brown which used deception to fool the Germans into thinking the attack would be from the north and pinpointed the German artillery positions so they could be negated before the attack. Fortress Blerick was taken with 22 dead and 100 casualties.*

Right: *Inside Blerick.*

Blerick

Below: *Bombarding Geysteren Castle are a Churchill and "Cuckoo," a 107th Pz Bde Panther captured during the battle of Overloon. It was used by the Coldstream Guards to bombard the castle, and later during Operation Blackcock where its maneuverability in icy conditions as well as the accuracy of its main armament were noticeable.*

1 *Winter camouflage for AFVs—not easy because of the shortage of both brushes and whitewash. The vehicle being whitewashed is a Humber scout car in the Maesyck area.*

2 *Artillery played an important part in the battles, but it also was an indiscriminate killer of civilians as well as enemies. Here 5.5in shells are prepared for howitzers of 236 Bty, 59th Med Regt, RA.*

3 *The end result of whitewashing. This Cromwell is moving up to take part in Operation Blackcock.*

4 *Members of the Tank Troop of Tac HQ 7th Armd Div Holland, Winter 1944/45.*

Below: *The gallant fight at Susteren as depicted in the* Illustrated London News. *B Coy 1/5th Queens Royal Regt hanging on grimly in the northern part of Susteren village as they waited for 1RTR to get across the Vloed Beek to support them. They were attacked by a battalion of infantry supported by six tanks, but managed to knock out two of them and to hold on until the tanks arrived.*

Operation Blackcock

Right and Below Right: *2 Devons take Echt and look for German stay-behind forces.*

Snow-suited troops of 131st Bde, 7th Armd Div, in universal carriers drive past German prisoners in Echt, January 18, 1945.

Right: *Operation Blackcock took place during January 1945. Largely overlooked by the history books because of its proximity to the Battle of the Bulge and the Rhine Crossings, it was a bitter little campaign that saw British XII Corps (7th Armd, 52nd Lowland, and 43rd Wessex) divisions drive back XII SS Korps strengthened by Fallschirmjäger-Regiment Hübner. The operation achieved its objectives in the face of strong opposition, the crucial battle being the attack on Sint Joost that took four attacks and the use of Crocodiles to clear the Fallschirmjäger opposition. With the Roer triangle clear, plans proceeded for the clearance of the Rhineland.*

Below Right: *A Cromwell Tank Crew of 7th Armoured eating lunch, note tankers' gear.*

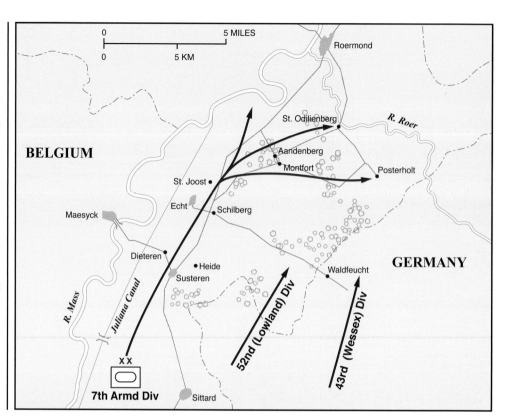

Above: *Men of 2nd Bn, Devonshire Regt clearing the town of Echt of the German rearguard, January 18, 1945 (see also pp170–171).*

Right: *The artificial moonlight battle for Montfort as depicted in the* Illustrated London News. *Tanks and infantry of the division attacking Montfort seized the outskirts but came up against fierce enemy resistance. The village was eventually occupied during the night of January 23–24.*

Crocodiles in support of the Rifle Brigade in action in Sint Joost, where there was heavy fighting on January 20–21. Fearful weapons, the Crocodiles had a flamethrower range of around 120 yards. The fuel—sufficient for 80 one-second bursts—was carried in a trailer behind the tank.

Left, Below Left, and Below: *Churchill tanks laden with 9th DLI infantry pass a knocked out German PaK40 7.5cm anti-tank gun as they enter Schilberg, January 20. Note that an Allied 75mm AP round has neatly perforated the gun's armored shield. This may well have been responsible for the dead German soldier lying by his gun. The battalion fought as part of the ground forces of Market Garden at Gheel before transferring to 131st Inf Bde, 7th Armd Div, fighting at the Roer Triangle and the town of Ibbenbüren. The battalion ended the war near Hamburg.*

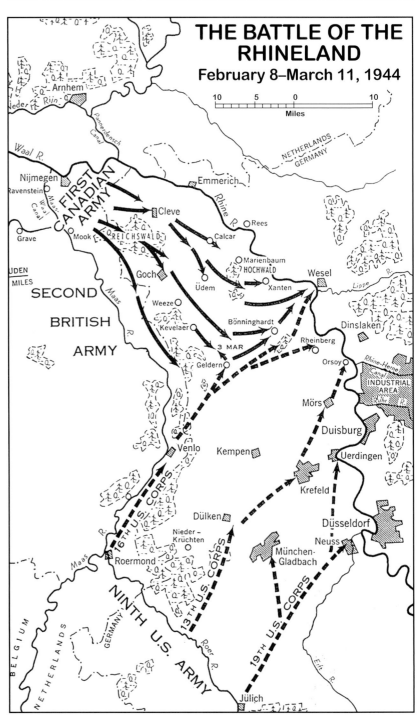

THE BATTLE OF THE RHINELAND
February 8–March 11, 1944

Top: *Venlo was the railhead at which the 107th Pz Bde arrived during Market Garden. On the eastern edge of the Meuse down river from Maastricht, its western suburb on the other bank, Blerick, fell in November 1944 (see p168).*

Above Right: *British troops in trenches at Blerick.*

Right: *Map showing the clearance of the Rhineland by Canadian First Army, British XXX Corps, and US Ninth Army, February 8–March 11, 1945. Operations Veritable (from the north) and Grenade (the Americans from the south) were planned to start simultaneously. Unfortunately, the Roer dams had not been captured and the Germans were able to flood the river. This halted the US portion of the operation for two weeks and Ninth Army was not able to start until February 23. One of the attacking units was the 30th Division—whom we last followed in the Ardennes.*

Between February 8 and 23 Operation Veritable made slow progress. The flooding of the Roer halted the US—southern—component (Operation Grenade) in its tracks, allowing the Germans to pull units north. Having started well, the weather, the water, and the mud conspired to slow progress—made even slower by a veteran defense. Masterminded by General der Infanterie Erich Straube, every village and town became a major obstacle and the Allies paid for every inch of ground gained. Starting from Mook and Groesbeek—scene of the 82nd Airborne's heroic defense on the flank of Market Garden—the advance through the Reichswald forest to Cleve and Goch saw heavy losses on both sides. A graphic example was at Moyland Wood where the 7th Canadian Inf Bde—comprising the "Water Rats" (the Royal Winnipeg Rifles), Regina Rifle Regt, and 1st Canadian Scottish—took on elements of 6th FJR Div and won out against fanatical defense. The final attack started on February 21 and made skilful use of supporting artillery, airpower (No. 84 Group, RAF), tanks (from the Sherbrooke Fusiliers), and Wasp flamethrowers (six each from the Winnipeg Rifles and Canadian Scottish) which were rotated to ensure three were at the front at all times.

Opposite, Top: *The Germans blew dikes on the River Rhine and the water levels rose steadily throughout the first few days of "Veritable." Here, a signals line party working along the the Nijmegen–Cleve road near Kranenburg. The main road became impassable to wheeled vehicles and all movement had to be switched to the roads closer to the Reichswald. The signallers are moving forward in amphibious Weasels and DUKWs.*

Opposite, Inset: *A knocked-out Valentine XI has succumbed to the rising waters along the same road just after the opening of the operation.*

Opposite, Bottom: *An infantryman of the US 78th Div surveys the cascading water tumbling down from the Schwammenauel Dam. German engineers had blown the valves and machinery in the dam to allow a measured but unstoppable flow of water down the Roer in order to keep its valley in a state of flood for as long as possible thus preventing the launch of the American attack across the river.*

Above: *Bren carriers of the Highland Light Infantry at Goch, February 25.*

Left: *Men of the 2nd Gordon Highlanders from 227th Bde 15th Scottish Div wait in their Kangaroos outside Kranenburg before the advance to Cleve.*

177

Above: *A party of VIPs in front of the Citadel at Jülich just after they had taken lunch in the ruined fortress. From left to right Maj-Gen. Raymond S. McLain (US XIX Corps), FM Bernard Montgomery (British 21st Army Group), Winston Churchill (British Prime Minister), Maj-Gen. Alvan C. Gillem (US XIII Corps) FM Alan Brooke (British Chief Imperial Gen Staff), and Lt-Gen. William H. Simpson (US Ninth Army).*

Below and Bottom: *Ninth Army (**Below**) and 2nd Armored shoulder patches.*

The reservoirs fed the River Roer for nearly two weeks before they began to dwindle, and as they did Gen. William Simpson's Ninth Army struck. A brilliant river crossing on February 23 saw a bridgehead carved out by Ninth Army's XIII (84th and 102nd Inf Divs) and XIX Corps (29th and 30th Inf Divs), and First Army's VII Corps (104th and 8th Inf Divs). The exploitation by armor—particularly 2nd "Hell on Wheels" Division—saw spectacular gains in a dynamic advance that did much to foster the credentials of Gen Simpson, Ninth's quietly understated Texan CG, who established a particularly good working relationship with his 21st Army Group commander, FM Montgomery. Monty said in a later letter to Simpson, "It has fallen to my lot to be mixed up with a good deal of fighting ... and the experience I have gained enables me to judge pretty well the calibre of Armies. I can truthfully say that the operations of the Ninth Army, since 23 Feb last, have been up to the best standards."

Further north, Operation Blockbuster, which started on February 26, was intended to kickstart the northern push to the Rhine. Again it started well, but bogged down in the Hochwald Gap where the Canadians won through in a battle that Royal Hamilton Light Infantry commander Brig-Gen. W.D. Whitaker dubbed "Canada's Hürtgen Forest."

The Rhineland campaign cost some 25,000 Allied casualties, but by its end, on March 10, the Allies were on the Rhine, over 50,000 Germans had been captured and around 40,000 killed or wounded.

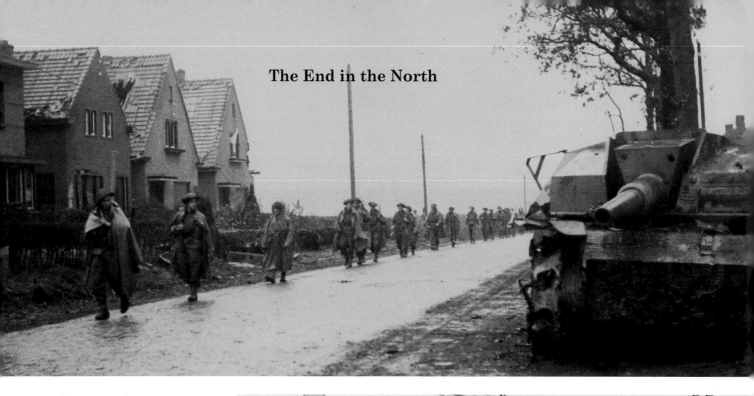

The End in the North

Above: *Canadian troops pass a Sturmhaubitze 42 at the end of the Scheldt clearing operation that had cost them over 4,000 casualties.*

Right: *Infantry of the Regiment de Maisonneuve moving through Holten to Rijssen, east of Deventer, April 9, 1945.*

Below Right: *The Canadian forces spent some time recovering after the Scheldt battles. There was a fillip in January when they were joined by Canadian troops from Italy, but the Germans were implacable in their continued defiance and right up to the end there was hard fighting. After the ceasefire, in the western Netherlands the priority was providing food for the starving Dutch population, many of them isolated in flooded villages*

Opposite:
A and B *The last months of the war saw Canadian forces fan out into the west and north of the Netherlands.*

C and D *The Canadian 1st Inf Div was tasked with liberating the west of the country advancing through Apeldoorn (**C**) and Amersfoort (**D**), where there was a concentration camp, the Polizeiliches Durchgangslager Amersfoort (Police Transit Camp Amersfoort), on its way to Rotterdam.*

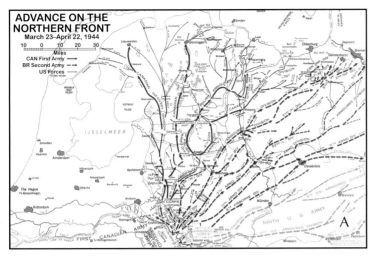

ADVANCE ON THE NORTHERN FRONT
March 23–April 22, 1944

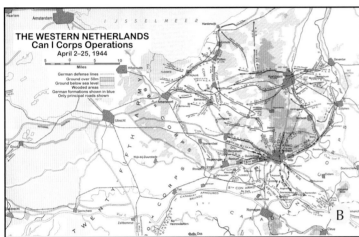

THE WESTERN NETHERLANDS
Can I Corps Operations
April 2–25, 1944

The final weeks of the war in the Low Countries were cruel for both the liberators and the liberated. The German forces—whose occupation had resulted in the deaths of 234,000 Dutch citizens—clung on till the bitter end. At Groningen, for example, a four-day battle (April 13–16) cost the Canadian 2nd Inf Div 209 casualties in the face of its SS defenders. In the west, by April 19, offensive operations on the I Corps front had virtually ceased for fear of further German flooding—but it would not be until May 5, at Wageningen a few miles west of Arnhem, that the Twenty-Fifth German Armee officially surrendered. Oberstgeneral Johannes Blaskowitz, the commander of forces in the Netherlands, signing the instrument of surrender in the Hotel de Wereld. Today the street is named General Foulkesweg after the Canadian I Corps commander who accepted the surrender. Prince Bernhard of the Netherlands was also present.

Below: *Canadian 4th Armd advanced north crossing the Twente Canal on April 3, moving into Germany. There was stiff fighting all the way, particularly around Oldenburg. The division was some 10 miles north of the town at the cease fire on May 5, 1945.*

It became obvious to the Allies that something had to be done to alleviate civilian suffering in late April 1945. On top of the rigors of war, the flooding of so much of the country and the harsh weather were factors, but the main reason for the "Hunger Winter" of 1944–45 in which around 20,000 died of starvation and related problems, was the German embargo on food transportation to the Western Netherlands. This followed a September rail strike—initiated at the start of Operation Market Garden—when it seemed that the war would be over soon.
 There was some relief from Sweden—under the Red Cross some ships were allowed to bring in flour to make "Swedish bread"—and Switzerland. The Allies became involved with Operations Manna (3,298 sorties by RAF Lancasters and Mosquitoes April 29–May 7) and Chowhound (2,268 sorties by USAAF B-17 Flying Fortresses, as seen at right, May 1–8) which dropped a total of over 11,000 tons. On top of this, Operation Faust saw 200 Allied trucks from the 21st Army Group deliver food to Rhenen behind German lines from May 2 onward. After the cease fire, the trucks went to Rotterdam.

A USAAF B-17G 44-46954 of the 569th Bomb Squadron out of RAF Framlingham drops food.

B In 2006 a memorial commemorating Operations Manna and Chowhound was set up near the A20 motorway at Terbregge, where 3,600 tons of food was dropped. Three artists were involved—Andre Dekker, Geert van der Camp, and Ruud Reutelingsberger— of the group Observatorium. The memorial symbolizes stacks of food parcels inside the cargo hold of Allied bombers.

C Buffaloes in the Netherlands— the LVTs were one of the few methods of transport that worked in the wet conditions.

D In the north and west, many cities saw little fighting but some were unlucky. Groningen had to endure four days of violence including artillery shelling and bombing, as this 1945 photo of the Grote Markt shows.

The Henri-Chapelle American Cemetery and Memorial lies east of Liege. It holds the graves of 7,992 American World War II soldiers and the names of 450 missing.

Chapter 7
REMEMBERING
THE DEAD

Arranging the identification and burial of soldiers in the field, handling their personal effects, and subsequently arranging for their interment in suitable cemeteries is an fundamental army requirement. For the US Army, this function was given to The Quartermaster General in 1861 and it has evolved since then. In World War II, the Graves Registration Section became responsible for recommending the location of cemeteries and the registration of graves.

A *A 26th Inf Div Graves Registration detail collects the dead after fighting in Luxembourg, January 16, 1945.*

B *90th Division graves at Bavinge, Luxembourg.*

C *3042nd Graves Registration Coy collects Allied and enemy dead just outside Bastogne.*

D and E *Margraten, near Maastricht, is the site of the Netherlands American Cemetery and Memorial—the only American military cemetery in the Netherlands. Established in 1960, it holds 8,301 burials and the names of 1,722 missing in action.*

This Page: *The Mardasson Memorial honors the memory of the 76,890 American soldiers who were wounded or killed during the Battle of the Bulge. Dedicated on July 16, 1950, the complex was designed by Architect Georges Dedoyard. The inner walls are covered with ten paintings from the battle; the outer crown is engraved with the names of the contemporary 48 US States, and the insignia of most participating battalions are shown on the walls.*

Above Right: *This eagle memorial commemorates the "Screaming Eagles"—the 101st Airborne Division—who were the primary defenders of the besieged city. Donated by the city of Bastogne and its inhabitants it can be found near the Mardasson Memorial and the text on the plaque reads:*
"May this eagle always symbolize the sacrifices and heroism of the 101st Airborne Division and all its attached units."

Below: *The star-shaped Mardasson Memorial at left is next door to the Bastogne War Museum which opened in 2014 and is well worth a visit.*

Above Left and Right: *The Luxembourg American Cemetery and Memorial was established on December 29, 1944, by the 609th Quartermaster Coy of the US Third Army. Gen. George S. Patton had his HQ in Luxembourg City. There are 5,076 burials here and the names of 371 of the missing. Rosettes mark the names of those since recovered and identified. Gen. Patton is buried here, too, as he wished, alongside his men of the Third Army.*

Right: *There are many British and Commonwealth cemeteries in the Low Countries. This one, at Overloon, contains 280 Commonwealth burials and one Dutch war grave.*

Left: *The distinctive architecture of a CWGC cemetery, with the Cross of Sacrifice as designed by Sir Reginald Blomfield. Hotton was the western limit of the German Ardennes offensive, and most of the burials date from then, although some of the 666 date from May 1940.*

Below Left: *The CWGC Holten Canadian War Cemetery near Deventer in the Netherlands contains 1,393 Commonwealth burials from World War II, most of whom died during the advance of the Canadian II Corps into northern Germany.*

Bottom Left: *Each year the people of the town of Hoevelaken in the Netherlands commemorate the death of a young Canadian from the Loyal Edmonton Regiment, who died in their village on April 19, 1945. Walter Strang had fought in Italy before being transferred to the Netherlands in 1945. Even at this late stage of the war, there was still heavy fighting, and in one engagement, on April 19, Walter Strang died, nine days before the ceasefire. To give a human face to their annual commemoration, in 1946 the townsfolk erected a monument with the inscription:*
"Here fell 19-4-'45 W. STRANG of the Canadian army, in his memory we honour our liberators."
In 2008 the monument was augmented with, as the Walter Strang website elucidates:
"a stainless steel plate will be placed behind the existing monument with a life-size picture of Walter Strang. This image is repeated, but then as a cut-out shape symbolising his sudden departure from life. The stainless steel symbolises his birthplace Glasgow ..."
Strang was interred in the Canadian War Cemetery at Groesbeek.

CREDITS

As always, loads of people helped with this book, in particular we'd like to thank Neil Powell of *www.battlefield historian.com* who supplied many of the photographs, the volunteers of STIWOT whose brilliant website *Tracesofwar. com* catalogs military memorials, monuments, museums and fortifications, and Warren Watson of *www.oldhickory30th.com* from whom the Dr. Van Heely's collection came. Thanks also to Mark Franklin for the maps, Peter Anderson and Richard Wood (of Wood's Tours), for many of the today photos, Elly for design and the helpful staff of NARA at College Park, MD.

As far as the photos go, the aerial photos are all by Leo Marriott. We've tried to identify below the copyright holders or providers of the photos: apologies if we've missed anyone.

Peter Anderson: 81B, 83B and inset x3, 84 inset, 85TL&TR, 88TL, CL&CR, 89B, 123 inset, 127, 131 CL&CR, 139CL, 143BL&BR, 144TR&CR, 164C, BL&BR, 170CL&BR, 173BR, 187TL.

Battlefield Historian: 13 (both), 19L, 23T, 24C&B, 25T&C, 26T, 27T&C, 30–31, 32CT, CB&B, 33 (all), 36B, 68T, 76BL&CL, 77BR, 80T, 83T, 83BR, 86 (all), 91 (both), 92B, 99TL, TR, CL&CR, 100CR, 102 (all), 103T, 106TR, 107T, 108T, 109CL, CR&BR, 110–111 (all), 115T, 116BL, 117T, 119 (both), 121B, 126TL, 131T&B, 133T, CR&BR, 134T&B, 135T, CR&B, 136T&B, 137TL, TR&CR, 140TL&TR, 141T, 142C&B, 147TL&TR, 148C&B, 149 (all), 154B, 155 (both), 175T, 176 (all), 177B, 178–179 (all), 186C.

Canadian Maps: 21 (inset B), 44TL (both), 54TR, 60CL&R, 61CL&R), 61B, 62 (all). © All rights reserved. *Official History of the Canadian Army in the Second World War Volume III*

The Victory Campaign The Operations in North-West Europe, 1944-1945 reproduced with the permission of DND/CAF 2014.
G. Forty Collection: 1, 4–5, 7 (inset A), 10T, 22L, 36CR, 38 (all), 40B, 41TR&CR, 41B, 52B, 54TL, 54C&B, 55C&B, 56 (both insets), 57 (inset), 59B, 60B, 61TR, 66 (both), 67, 68 (inset), 69 (all), 70, 74C, 76 (inset), 77T and inset, 78–79, 84BL, 85BL&BR, 93BC, 94T, 95TL&TR, 95B, 96TL, 99B, 100T&B, 103B, 105T, 106TL, 106B, 120B, 137BR, 142B, 150 (all), 152–153, 154T, 158 (all), 159B, 162–163, 166CL, 169 (all). 170TL, CL, CR&BR, 172 (all), 173T, B&CL, 181T&C, 187TR.
Dalton Einhorn: 120 (inset top).
Dr. Van Heely 113th Field Artillery Photograph Collection: 72–75, 128–129.
Library of Congress: 121T.
NARA: 6–7, 7 (inset), 8, 10B, 11 (both), 12 (all), 14–15, 16, 17 (both), 18, 19R, 20–21, 21 (inset T&C), 22AL&BL, 23B, 25B, 26BL&BR, 28–29, 34TR&BR, 35 (all), 36TL&R, 36CL, 37 (both), 39 (I–K), 40TL, 41C, 45C&B, 46CL, 49TR, 51T, 60T, 64B, 71, 80B, 82T, 87 (all), 88TR, 89T, 90 (all), 94B, 96TR, 112–113, 115BL&BR, 116TL, 117B, 118 (all), 122B, 123T, 123B, 124T, 130T, 132C, 136C, 138B, 139B, 140B, 142T, 145C&B, 146B, 148T, 156, 157B, 159T&C, 160T&C, 165B, 166T&B, 168 (all), 174TR, 175B, 177T, 180 (all), 181B, 182–183, 185 inset, 186 (A and B).
Marco Ritman, Venray: 166CR.
Traces of War: 63TL (Jeroen Koppes), 63BR (Anneke Moerenhout), 93 (BL, BC, BR all Barry van Veen), 97 (inset Barry van Veen), 116 (D–F all Jeroen Koppes), 126 (inset TR Jeroen Koppes), 133 (H Jeroen Koppes), 134 (E Jeroen Koppes), 146 (insets both Barry van Veen), 175C (Barry van Veen), 182L (Vincent Krabbendam).

US Center of Military History: 31T, 33, 38H, 40TR, 41TL, 71 inset, 81T, 131B, 132T, 138T, 145T, 146T, 150TL, 165T.
Richard Wood: 95C, 100BL, 104BL&BR, 107B, 109 (all modern images), 124–125B, 125 inset.
via Wikicommons: 34TL Captmondo, 36CR Kokin, 40B AlfvanBeem; 48 inset Michel wal, 61T Tabercil; 63CL Paul Hermans; 63CR RoschM; 64 inset Paul Hermans, 65CL Miho, 65BL Gouwenaar, 65BR Paultregouet, 106TL and 106B (Havang(nl), 132 BL&BR Zirguezi, 133CL Les Meloures, 135C (Jean-Pol Grandmont), 157T Alaging, 179 MrInfo2012, 189T Les Meloures, 189C JanB46, 189B Apdency, 190 H. van der Meer.
Others: 32BC *www.82nd engineers.org/*; 32T, From a watercolor by Capt. O.N. Fisher in *The Canadian Army at War*.

Bibliography

Many internet sites have proved helpful including: *www.atlantikwall.mynetcologne.de/Atlantikwall/index. html*—a fantastic resource for information on the Atlantic Wall defenses, as is *www.bunkerpictures.nl/*. Other great sites include: info about Brigade Piron—*www.brigade-piron.be*; the US Army Center of Military History—*www.history.army.mil*, from which one can read the excellent "Green Books," the US Army in World War II Series; and *www.ibiblio.org/hyperwar/UN/Canada/* where official Canadian histories are available. Patton's After Action Report on Third Army's progress is essential reading and other real books used include the unparalleled After the Battle series: *D-Day, Rückmarsch, Battle of the Bulge, Operation Market Garden*; specific titles from Osprey's Fortress, New Vanguard, and Campaign series; and numerous histories—*The Forgotten Battle* covering Overloon and the Maas Salient (by Altes and Veld) is excellent, as are Whitaker's *Rhineland: The Battle to End the War*, Moulton's *Battle for Antwerp*, Bob Kershaw's *It Never Snows in September* and more recent *A Street in Arnhem*, and Ken Ford's *Assault Crossing: The*

River Seine 1944. For depth of study, the *Duel in the Mist* coverage of Leibstandarte in the Ardennes is hard to beat. George Forty's range of titles has also proved helpful, particularly *Fortress Europe, The Armies of George Patton*, and *The Reich's Last Gamble*. There are a wealth of personal memoirs and unit histories available—one of the best is Don Fox's excellent *Patton's Vanguard* covering the exploits of 4th Armored.

Below: *Ysselsteyn near Venray is the location of the largest German War Cemetery and contains the graves of 31,598 German war dead, all but 85 from World War II. It is administered by the German War Graves Commission, the Volksbund Deutsche Kriegsgräberfürsorge.*

INDEX